A is for ... Action!

A short time ago I discovered that there was very little that painted an accurate picture of the role of the humble cover supervisor. A typical example of this is "Cover Work *should* be set in readiness for the cover supervisor to deliver the lesson." However in this particular text, it never explains what to do when you've had to dash from one side of the building to the other during lesson change over. You've arrived to your next cover lesson at the same time as the pupils, no work has been set, and you can't leave a class full of excitable 14 year olds unsupervised, to toddle off to find the Head of English to locate the cover work for that lesson. Typically a lot of the literacy regarding cover supervisors is idealistic, not thought through and generally written by people who have no experience of actually performing the job.

With this in mind, I decided that ACTION had to be taken. I wrote this book and had taken the manuscript to an educational book publisher, where several people (including a retired teacher and a deputy head) criticised the integrity, purpose and content of the script. Their opinions were based on a lack of experience and misunderstanding of the role. Based on these opinions, the publisher rejected my book! You only need to search the internet, to see the number of cover supervisors needed by agencies. It's with this in mind, these people at least need some guidance in the classroom. And this is where this book comes in, I hope the book is of some assistance to you.

> From one cover supervisor to another.... I hope the book offers support, practical advice and ideas that will support you in most situations

Acronyms, jargon...

Schools by their very nature are hectic, chaotic and busy places, where staff need to communicate a lot of information very quickly to each other. And as a result, over many years they have developed their own language, complete with jargon, acronyms and abbreviations.

Below is a list of common terms

CS	Cover Supervisor
TA	Teaching Assistant
HLTA	Higher Level Teaching Assistant
HOY	Head Of Year
HOD	Head Of Department
AFL	Assessment For Learning
AOL	Assessment Of Learning
SIMS	School Information Management system
Starter	First activity of the lesson
Extension	Extra activity for pupils who complete
VLE	Virtual Learning Environment
IWB	Interactive White Board (Smart Board)
Plenary	Final activity of the lesson

A to Z for Cover Supervisors

The pocket companion for *all*
Cover Supervisors in the classroom

Wendy D. Ward

Dedication

A massive thank you to both Brenda and Louise
who originally saw the potential in me

For my gorgeous boyfriend Scott, who never
stopped believing in his little Wou Wou

And to my dearest Sprocket who
never left my side while I wrote

Ability Levels

Most classes are grouped based on ability (or not), gender or even in some cases by personalities (where some pupils have either been moved "up" or "down" to split up a bad cluster of pupils). As a cover supervisor you won't know how it's setted until you're actually in the lesson. Even class codes on the cover list will not always give away any clues. The only exception to this is with physical education when it's a practical lesson, where these are normally grouped based on gender.

You may think that higher ability groups will be easier, however think again! Their reasons for avoiding working may be more convincing, and plausible. They tend to chatter, and have developed more manipulative ways to dodge the work that's been set. This can be described as low level disruption.

Lower ability groups, in some cases can only be described as entering a wild zoo for an hour. Behaviour can be a problem, encouraging these pupils to work is going to be difficult (even for their regular teacher). These groups tend to collaborate together, and refuse to work as a whole. When trying to motivate these pupils to work, they often reply "why should I do it, when no one else is?" These types of groups tend to have many covers, as their regular teacher have chosen to arrange meetings for this lesson, or are absent due to "illness".

> Be realistic, you'll never get the same level of respect or behaviour from pupils. Sometimes it's just enough to ensure their safety, learning will not always take place

Agencies

Just type the words cover supervisor in to a search engine, and you're bombarded with various agencies wanting cover supervisors.

For some people, working for an agencies definitely has many benefits. Agency work offers flexibility and freedom. Some people may have unpredictable commitments such as health problems or caring for a family member, where they have to be flexible regarding work. Accepting work on a daily basis can be useful for them. Other people enjoy the freedom of going to different schools and gaining valuable experience. And, of course if you don't like a school, you needn't go back.

However, there are some drawbacks for working for an agency. At the start of the academic year (September and October time), it can be extremely quiet and work will be light. Unlike, school based cover supervisors, you will not be paid through the school holidays. To get around this, you'll have to be good at financial planning, or getting a second job may be necessary to get you through. Additionally, finding your way around each school can be problematic, but most schools issue supply staff with a map.

Whether you work for an agency or are based in one school, the role of the cover supervisor is still the same. Chances are, the cover work will be poor and the behaviour of the pupils will be less than perfect.

> Think about your own personal circumstances and then decide if an agency or based in one school suits you

Asking for help

This page is for both the cover supervisor and pupils alike. Respectfully, both groups are reluctant in asking for assistance for quite different reasons.

The cover supervisor is essentially performing the same role of a teacher (although as a one off) in delivering a lesson – the teacher is considerably more experienced to stand at the front of this particular class, know in advance what the lesson is about and fully understand the subject. The cover supervisor is at a substantial disadvantage, especially when you also consider the pupils behaviour as well. So with all this, the cover supervisor has two distinct weaknesses, it is ok to ask for help. Do not be a shamed.

Now, as for the pupils, they are quite a different species. Some pupils can be hesitant to ask for help. The reasons behind this could be one of many. Simply put, you're a stranger, some pupils (who are children after all) can still be a bit timid and shy around new people. Another reason could be that they don't want to be seen as the geek of the class, who is trying to work while the rest of the class are trying to do as little as possible.

To overcome this problem, when the class is on task (or as many pupils as possible), go around each table. Here, you can either motivate them to work, repeat the instructions of the task if needed, or just reassure them that what they're doing, is on the right track.

Ask for help – this is the message to remember yourself, and to encourage pupils to do the same

Assertiveness

Assertiveness sits neatly between being passive and being aggressive. As a cover supervisor you will have to confidently communicate what you wish the pupils to do in a positive way without coming across as being bossy. A fine balance, wouldn't you say?

If you can imagine some stranger entering the class room and being told that you *will* do the work, then you can guess the response of the pupils. Equally looking scared and timid as you enter the room, will only give the message that you're a walk over, and let's party!

Assertiveness allows the cover supervisor to have a presence in the classroom where pupils take notice of them. The question I hear you asking is how to become assertive? I have two answers, the first is that you pretend until it comes and secondly become more experienced in the class room. Assertiveness is linked with being confident, and this comes with time.

Body language is vital, be open, walk tall and look at pupils when talking to them. Tell pupils to do a task, never ask. An example of this "please can you do..." this is like your pleading or begging the pupils to do it. "This task needs to be completed by the end of the lesson" this is much better because it's polite, firm and concise.

If you can, observe both experienced teachers and cover supervisors. Watch how assertive they are, is there anything you can pick up from them?

Assessment

As a cover supervisor, you should never be ask to assess work completed by pupils. Teachers have been extensively trained on how to use their professional judgement and are able to see if pupils meet the assessment criteria or not.

With this in mind, I have included it because it is a word that is banded around school a great deal. At least if you can understand the concept of it, it may help you in future roles.

Assessment is a judgement which is made against a set of statements. You have to be qualified to make that judgement. It can take place at the start of the year, this acts as a marker to show what level the pupils are starting from. Another assessment will take place (either at the end of term or at the end of the year) these results can be compared with the original levels. The difference of these levels will show the amount of progress that has been made. This is really important because most teachers are measured professionally on the progress made by each pupil in their groups. Scary prospect hay?

The only task that cover supervisors can do is to invigilate a controlled assessment. In other words, supervise pupils performing a test in the classroom. At the end of the lesson, hand over the test papers to a teacher in person – never leave the papers unattended. This is where your dealings finish, never mark them.

You can assess pupil's behaviour, (it was good or bad) but please note this is only against your own personal standards

Atmosphere

The atmosphere that a classroom has is vital for the productivity of the pupils. As a cover supervisor you are limited to what you can do regarding the room. There isn't a lot you can do with an unloved classroom where displays are hanging off the boards and the window blinds are so shredded that they're letting the sun light through, and dazzling both you and the pupils.

However, you can control the temporary atmosphere by being positive and happy. When the pupils enter the room and you're smiling and happy to see them, (rather than looking angry and aggravated) it really sets the tone, and you are more likely to have a good lesson.

Pupils are as much to blame for setting the atmosphere as you. If, in their previous lesson something has happened, feelings can run over into your lesson. Your role in this situation is to calm it down and dilute their feelings during the lesson – difficult, I agree. Depending on the group, you have two choices. Either let the pupil talk to you about it, they may just want to talk to somebody and let off steam. Or discourage any talk about the issue at all, and hope they will forget about it, allowing you to get on with the current lesson. The atmosphere of the classroom, has been lately described as a climate for learning, where it covers both the physical aspects of the room and attitudes of all within it.

No matter how bad the previous lesson, let it go - and move on. If you don't, each lesson will only get worse and worse. The present class deserve better

Bad Behaviour

Fact: you will see a lot of bad behaviour as a cover supervisor. The reason for this is that you're not bad at your job (but this could be a possibility), but it starts with the pupils and how you deal with their behaviour. Simply put, they can misbehave with you because there is no come back. Unlike their regular teacher who has frequent contact with their parents, additionally you may not have access to their contact details. This makes you powerless – and they know it.

With this in mind, don't accept bad behaviour! "Set your stall out" right from the start. Be assertive, but firm. For example, when you're explaining the task and the group of girls are whispering at the back, stop what you're saying, and look at them. They'll soon stop, due to the peer pressure. This also sends a clear message to the rest of them. Tackle the low level disruption, this should prevent small problems growing into larger ones during the lesson.

If you're based in one school or are linked to an agency, try to follow the behaviour policy. Generally, they are all very similar, where the pupil receives a number of chances or warnings before moving up to the next sanction. This allows the pupil to consider what they have done, and gives them a chance to improve their behaviour. Read the policy and use the phrases and terms within it, this helps to maintain the consistency within the school.

Never make threats, such as giving out detentions and calling home unless you're willing to go through with it yourself

Bag of Tricks

This is probably the most important thing that you have to help you. Being organized in the classroom shows that you mean business and you can be seen as a good role model. Within your bag of tricks should be a variety of things that you can use at a moment's notice.

The bag itself shouldn't be an expensive one, but big enough for all your equipment including an A4 file. It should contain a number of pens, pencils, rulers, erasers and other such stationary that pupils can borrow if they need to. In addition to this, a small packet of tissues, board marker pens, a cloth (to wipe off the marker pen) a wad of both A4 plain and lined paper (an A4 file to keep it neat), and a selection of school forms, for example "out of class passes", and behaviour slips.

Furthermore, it's probably an advantage to collect ideas of tasks and activities from previous classes that you've covered. This is handy when the work is "light" and you need something else for the pupils to do. I've learnt from past experiences that if a class is sat without any work, they will become bored and eventually disruptive. It is far easier to set extra work, rather than to calm down 24 fractious pupils.

A memory stick can be useful, for setting up PowerPoints. I have a template already set up, where I only need to input the date, title and an explanation of the task, after this I display it on the interactive white board to show the pupils.

> Think like a squirrel. Start collecting ideas and lesson plans. Some activities can be used in a number of lessons

Balance

The role of a cover supervisor is very much like walking on a tight rope, in more than one sense.

Initially, on your job description it will state that you're merely a teaching assistant at level 3, but as far as teaching assistants, cover supervisors have a lot more responsibility.

Secondly, colleagues are still unsure of the role. Support staff see cover supervisors more as a teacher. Teachers see the role, as an unqualified teacher and don't consider the problems that leaving poor cover work can lead to.

What's more the pupils see cover supervisors as a teacher, but with less "power" – qualifications don't enter in their equation.

The true balancing act is trying to keep the peace and maintaining good behaviour while still keeping the pupils on your side. Preserving pupil cooperation is vital for a cover supervisor, pupils will either choose to do the work or not. Never go into a classroom wanting to be friends with them, in hope that they'll like you and *possibly* do as you say. Neither, go in as a sergeant major figure, shouting out orders. Remember you have a job to do, you need to issue the work, and ensure the pupils complete it. Be assertive, tell the pupils what is expected of them, both academically and behaviourally. Be clear with them that the same rules apply, even though their regular teacher is absent.

> Getting the right balance, develops over time. The more you cover lessons the easier it will become

Bank of Resources

Why do cover supervisors need a bank of resources? In an ideal world, we shouldn't. However for example, when half the English department is off, and the head of the department has to set work for 27 lessons for a variety of ages and abilities during form time – it's fair to say that the cover work will not be as "comprehensive" as it should be.

I'm not saying that you should have 28 copies of every worksheet that you have ever come across – for "just in case". Some of the problems linked with this idea, is that you'll end up with arms that belong to Geoff Capes (World's strongest man in the 1980's) as you have to carry them around, and the amount of paper you'll use – it's just not environmentally friendly, and you may never even use the worksheets.

The best resource that a cover supervisor can have is a physical file, you may not have access to a computer, so don't rely on your memory stick. The file is a place where you can keep lesson fillers that can fit most subjects. The best "fillers" shouldn't need much time to set up, or require any unusual resources other than those found in a normal classroom.

Normally at the start of every academic year it's very quiet for cover supervisors. Use this time to search the net and find activities that can work for you (you have to be confident to use them) and the type of pupils that you'll come across.

> Don't be put off by looking at websites aimed at teachers. When covering a lesson – you are replacing a teacher so you need access to the same sort of resources

Beliefs & Values

Once again, there are two sides to this topic. Whatever your beliefs or values are, they need to stop at the classroom door. You have to remain impartial, and neutral - you can't push your opinions onto pupils. These are young people who have yet to form their own. You may agree or disagree with their thoughts, but they have a right to have them. Generally speaking, politics (governmental or at a school level), religion, personal sexual matters or anything promoting illegal activities should be avoided in the classroom.

The other side of this topic is that of the pupil. Of course they have beliefs and values, but are not as tactful as (some) adults to know when to shut up about them. Some of these opinions are merely those of their parents. Additionally, these opinions can be racially motivated and can cause huge problems such as bullying in the classroom. Regarding this problem, it needs to be challenged immediately. As we all live in a multi-national society, there is no place for these opinions.

Subjects such as Religious Education/Studies are loaded with ethics and dilemmas, which are designed to make the pupils think and form an opinion for themselves. Within these lessons, a lot of debate will happen, and you may get involved. Depending on the emotional intelligence of the class, I would bounce the question back at the class, this helps you remain unbiased and won't upset any one.

| If you believe that what you're going to say is going to be controversial – then don't say it |

Be Prepared

Simply put, expect the unexpected. Don't think that your lesson will go without a hitch. Things that can go wrong, will go wrong at some point. Expect pupils arriving late, no work set, a fight starting, a stink bomb being let off, a fire drill, and so on. In each of these problems, your aim is to settle down the pupils as quickly as possible, and start working again. Though, that is easier said (or written) then done. Pupils don't like surprises or change. Any changes to their normal routine may send them in to an uncontrollable frenzy, even having a cover supervisor for their lesson can push them over the edge.

Anything that happens such as a fight or a fire drill will cause an element of excitement. During the event stay calm, don't make a fuss or panic, this will only cloud your judgement. Part of your role is to protect and safeguard the pupils in your care. You may have to make vital decisions on the spot regarding your class.

Some pupils may have "forgotten" their writing equipment, they'll ask to go to the next classroom for a pen (and kill some time out of lesson by talking to their friends). Disappoint them, by dipping your hand into your bag and lending them a pen. This also shows that you mean business and you expect them to work – don't give them an excuse to avoid working.

Consider the possible things that could hinder your lesson, and contemplate how to deal with that with as little fuss as possible

Be Professional

Dress appropriately. This is difficult for a cover supervisor, within one day you could cover a PE lesson (where you'll need your coat if it's outside), and then a wood work lesson followed by an academic based lesson such as maths. Smart but comfortable is the rule.

Follow the school rules and procedures. The pupils expect it, if you don't you're going to make problems for yourself. Pupils will know they don't have to behave because you don't follow the rules.

You may already, but respect all staff. This includes all senior management (regardless of what you think of them) down to the cleaners. Each member of staff is important, and for a school to work efficiently we all need to work together. Besides, you never know when you need their assistance.

Additionally, pupils need to be respected. No matter how annoyed they make you feel, you have to remember where you are and restrain yourself if needed.

Regardless of what role you have in school, you have to be seen as a role model on how to behave. This means, not swearing, chewing gum or using mobile phones if these are band within the school.

If you live locally to school, you have to behave in a certain way "out of hours". There is a chance that you may get spotted by pupils, or parents. So be careful if you like visiting your local pub!

Be professional is about behaving correctly, this will encourage pupils to behave appropriately

Body Language

This is very important! Even though we are in fount of a group of children – regardless of their ages, they are extremely good at subconsciously reading body language.

When you're at the front of the class, you cannot be timid or shy. Some classes will devour you for breakfast, if you don't take control. Your body language (as well as being assertive) will tell the class that you're in charge, and what you say goes.

If you can, stand at the door of the classroom and greet all pupils. This isn't always possible, but always arrive to class with a smile.

Don't sit and hide behind the teacher's desk during the lesson. The desk acts as a barrier, once the class is on task, walk around the room. Be high profile, this also prevents trouble from occurring within the lesson, because you're never too far away.

When explaining the task to the class, use the whole of the front of the classroom. Walk around, use all the space, for that lesson – the classroom belongs to you. This shows you are confident in the role.

Never cross your arms. This can be intimidating and aggressive in the wrong situation, in others it can be another barrier – a sign of weakness. As with all body language, keep it open.

I have just scratched the surface regarding body language here. If you're interested search the internet, and talk to teachers

Calmness

Being calm shows restraint and control. Pupils will see the cover supervisor as a bit of a novelty. Something to have a bit of fun with. Part of this will include trying to press your buttons and making you lose your temper. Some pupils, get a kick out of staff losing it, making a scene or having a break down.

Before you get to the point of losing your temper, take a deep breath, count to ten or whatever you need to do to calm down. If you can remain calm (or at least show it on the outside) it shows that you're in control and can handle the problem. Once the pupils know that it is pointless to continue– they will submit. If not the next stage is to put the pupil through the behaviour policy, this might result in removing that pupil from your room. Some pupils like to push their luck with the cover supervisor.

There are other situations when remaining calm is essential. If a fight brakes out, you cannot panic. You are still expected to keep in control, do not get involved to split them up (union's recommendation) but do your best to verbally stop the fight. Separate the fighters, one in another room. And then get the rest of the class back on task. If pupils see you flustered, the rest of the class will lose their trust in you.

Always take time out afterwards to calm down properly.

Plan ahead. Consider what you would do if pupils tried to push your buttons, how would you deal with it in a calm way? It's easier to do this when you're thinking clearly. If it happens, you'll then know what to do

Carrot versus Stick

This topic is the same as the "wind and the sun fable", where one thing competes against the other for the same end result. In the fable, it's to take the coat off the travellers back, in the classroom it's to get the pupils to settle down and work.

Many schools on a whole focus on reward (which is the sun) rather than sanctions (which is the wind). It encourages positivity, and is more inclusive and focuses on the majority of pupils who are well behaved. Some schools use a stamp system, or stickers where pupils collect them and they earn a prize at the end of the week or term.

The moral of the fable, it's easier to get what you want through kindness. People (especially children) like praise. As a cover supervisor you may not be able to give out stamps or stickers (if you're from an agency for the day for example). But remain positive and give praise and pay attention to those who deserve it. The "naughty" pupils desire attention. If they want it, they'll have to behave – if they don't behave use the behaviour policy.

I wouldn't advise on giving sweets out for good behaviour (or badly behaved pupils behaving less badly). Most schools are healthy schools, where chips are band and fizzy pop has vanished. Sweets may go against school policies. Besides it could work out very costly, when pupils expect them when they see you.

As hard as it is – experiment. Don't shout, but praise and see what happens

Challenge

I'll let you into a little secret. The word challenge (in any context) means it's either hard or difficult! So, most of us would agree that working as a cover supervisor is a challenge. It takes a special person to do this job over any length of time.

Some of the biggest problems (or challenges) that you'll fine as a cover supervisor is the lack of work left by the teachers. It's a fact that most teachers (who are setting their own work) will not be as thorough as they may be when their setting their own lessons. And, if other teachers set the work for others – it won't be ideal – it may be a standalone lesson, and these come with their own problems.

Another challenge, is other staff. The role of the cover supervisor is a unique one. Many staff have no idea of the daily problems that are faced by cover supervisors. Staff will either try to unofficially delegate more duties on to cover supervisors, or completely undermined us. In both cases – bite your tongue, and deal with it professionally.

Pupils are the other challenge. Some will try to course you a lot of problems and simply will not cooperate. No matter how much experience you have – these never go away. The year 11 pupils just get replaced by another generation of "ratbags" in year 7. They will always be "ratbags" in every year group. Only the faces change, but they all behave in the same way. Luckily, it's an easy problem to solve, we can refine how we deal with the problem until we get it right and become than expert at behaviour.

> It's not an easy job – but the more effort you put in, the easier it gets, as you gain experience

Child Development

Regardless of what age you are working with, children are developing – learning about the world around them. Primary school pupils tend to be selfish and think only about themselves. When these children attend secondary school – they have a need to "belong" and need to find a niche group to fit in. When working in primary schools – you'll be running around the classroom helping each child. Yet, in secondary school that very same child who looked at you for help previously, now look at you as you're something they have stepped in. And this is typical of some teenagers.

The point is, regardless of how good you are – you can't fight against nature. Children have to go through this change before they reach adulthood. Some of these changes are physical, but a lot of changes occur in the brain. In adolescents the brain (explained in its simplest form) rewires its self in preparation for adulthood. In this process, many things "go off line" when their being rewired. This explains the irrational behavior of teenagers.

You may only see that particular child once, but you'll see hundreds of children going through the same thing. With this in mind, accept that it's a tough time for them but never accept bad behaviour. Teenagers still require the structure of school, as school maybe the only place that is settled. With the advent of social network sites – they tend to fall out/break up, make up and become best friends all in one day.

> I have only scratch the surface of child development - to understand the subject further have a look on the internet, talk to professionals or get a book from the library

Child Protection

This is extremely important, given all the recent stories in the media. Every effort has been made so that any accusation made, is taken seriously - regardless of how unbelievable it may sound at the time.

If a child approaches you and discloses a piece of information, listen to them and never question them. Also never promise that you'll keep it a secret. Once you have written down everything that the child has said – without putting phrases such as "in my opinion..." just write the facts. This information then needs to be given to the child protection officer, where they can deal with it. Do not expect to hear anything after that.

You may also be asked to write a statement based on observations that you have noticed about a child. For example if a particular child is consistently dirty, or has started to behave differently, or even has bruises on their body. The problem with these is that they may point to neglect or abuse, but there could be other problems that have led to the child becoming like this. Your role is just to report what you see, and that is it.

The guidelines and laws of child protection are changing all the time. So keep up with all the training that is offered. Please don't be in the situation where you knew "that child", who appears on the television – where you believe that you could have done something that could have put a stop to their suffering.

> Read the policy on child protection at school, and then follow it

Classroom Conflictions

This page is about how to tackle bullying in the classroom. In the absence of their regular teacher – the dynamics change considerably. Whereas their normal teacher knows their groups inside out – and the group will know the behaviour expectations to behave to – if not it can be dealt with, by contacting home. This is a luxury that you don't have, and the pupils know it.

In regards off bullying it can be seen as any unwanted attention (physically, emotionally or electronically) aimed at any other person that doesn't want it.

Every child is different, some children find it hard to accept difference. For example pupils who have SEN or are from another country tend to be prone to bullying. They can find it difficult to stand up for themselves. As a cover supervisor you have to enforce the expectation, that everyone is different, and that is no reason to make "fun of them". It's all about maintaining the rules, and bulling is not acceptable.

If it occurs in your lesson, try and stop it immediately, never take sides. The pupils in question may need to be separated. You can move pupils to sit one at the front and one at the back, or if you know that isn't going to work, consider moving one to another classroom "to calm down".

Remember what it was like when you were at school if you were ever bullied? It's no fun – so always take it seriously when covering

Comfort Breaks

Comfort break? In other words going to the toilet. This is something that is for you, as well as all the pupils you meet. This can be a problem, when nature calls. I'm going to be realistic, we all have to eat and drink, and of course the inevitable has to happen.

Lead by example! Only go for a comfort break out of lesson time, or when you're not covering. At all costs, avoid leaving a class unsupervised because you have to go for a comfort break. You could end up losing your job!

As for the pupils, never let them go when they have just come in from either break or lunch time. Their free time, is their time (just like ours) to do the necessities in order to function properly in lesson. Particularly in secondary school, they have to learn skills that they'll need, when they start work. And this is one skill – some employers will not accept their employees going to the loo, outside their allotted breaks and lunch times.

If a pupil is persistently asking to go to the toilet, after you have repeatedly said "no", then reluctantly let them go. But always issue them with a note, this is in line with safeguarding.

Some pupils will resort to some underhanded tricks to go. I've known teenage girls ask male staff (teachers, as well as cover supervisors) that they must go "because they are on their period". Teenage girls know about the embarrassment factor. It's impossible for men to say no to this. = rock and hard place?

Lead by example, and cut down on the coffee if needed!

Communication

This is a fundamental skill that cover supervisors need. This starts right at the start of the day, when you receive that phone call from the agency or when you pick up the cover list for the day.

When you enter the class and find the cover lesson plan, this is a form of communication. This is the teacher telling you what they want you to do with the class. This can be the start of the problems. The information that is available to you can be very limited. The lesson plan, may only be one sentence! This is where your preparation comes in!

Once the lesson has finished, try (if time allows) to leave feedback to the teacher. This allows the teacher to know where the class has got up to, and any problems that need chasing up. Additionally if the pupils know that there is some form of communication, they will think twice about "playing up". Feedback can either be given in written form (hand written on the plan or email) or verbally if you see the teacher face to face.

When stood at the front of the class, ensure that you can be heard, and that the type of words that you use are appropriate for the age group you are working with. Some problems can occur if the pupils don't understand the explanation of the task, they may become frustrated and start misbehaving.

| Don't waffle, or use bigger words then needed – you're not impressing anyone |

Confidence

In order to be a cover supervisor you have to be extremely confident. As a cover supervisor, being confident allows you to do your job well. After all, it has to take a special type of person to enter a strange class room, not knowing the group of pupils and be assertive enough to convince the group to work.

When you first start, confidence will not always be there. If this happens, pretend! Pupils will never know the difference. Act as though you are confident, over time the confidence will come, and you won't need to pretend.

If you're struggling with gaining confidence, watch other cover supervisors and teachers in lessons, and even talk to them. They will offer help and ideas to overcome your shyness.

Confidence is a collective effort that uses assertiveness, body language, facial expressions, experience and being prepared. It does take time to become self-confident but it is worth it in the end. Additionally it can also help you outside the classroom, in your personal life.

The advantages for being confident in the classroom includes, it offers pupils peace of mind and are assured that there in safe hands. Some pupils can feel insecure when their regular teacher is absent. Of course, you can't replace them but you can ensure that their needs of safety and security are met.

> Watch how other cover supervisors come across as being confident, and try to adapt it to suit you

Consistency

Children like routines and consistencies. When pupils see you time and time again, but in different lessons – it's important to maintain the same set of standards. This can be difficult as the week goes on and you get tired and stressed. Although if you soldier on, it will get easier throughout the year.

If you can continue cracking down on the low level disruption, this should prevent bigger problems from kicking off such as fighting and vandalism. Low level disruption includes, such things as talking when you are, and chewing gum. It'll stop eventually, when pupils know you won't put up with it. I write from personal experience, the hardest part of this is upholding the consistency from day to day and week to week. I've learnt just to knuckle down and persevere. When it gets to the last few weeks of term, it becomes easy as the pupils know what you expect, and know it's just easier to behave.

In addition to personal consistency, you also have to maintain the rules of the school. Sometimes, you may agree or disagree with the rules, or believe that their too strict or not enough, this is your opinion, but you still have to follow them. If you work for an agency it can be difficult remembering the exact details of the rules of each school. However most agencies will have allocated maybe 4 or 5 schools that you go to all the time. This eliminates the confusion.

What you put in, you'll get out. It isn't easy "setting out your stall" and keeping up to it. But if you want to progress on to teaching – its good practice

Cover Manager

This person probably has the most stressful job in the school (next to cover supervisors, of course). They have to get in early, take all the phone calls from all the staff who won't be in for that day, enter this information on to SIMS, assign internal cover supervisors to lessons, and phone agencies for additional staff, and print out all the paper work ready for the cover staff to pick up - all before school starts.

Having a good cover manager can make all the difference. They will lookout for their staff, and ensure that all messages and lesson changes are passed on quickly. They will also understand the layout of the school, and will try to get your classes close to each other – this saves you valuable time during lesson change over.

Normally, the cover manager will be the line manager for the cover supervisors. This can be useful. The manager should know the strengths and weaknesses of all their staff, and place each cover supervisor in the most appropriate lessons.

Above all else, the cover manager should share out the cover lessons equally within the team. And when cover supervisors are not being used to cover, they can be used to support other cover supervisors. This also doubles up on observing them, where they can swap ideas and lesson activities.

If you have a good cover manager – consider yourself lucky

Cover Supervisor

The role came about when the government (2008) decided that teachers should have more of a work life balance. In order to do this, a white paper was submitted that suggested that there was a number of tasks that teachers do, that could be completed by support staff. Previously teachers could be used during their PPA lessons for cover. Now, teachers can only be used for a maximum of 3 lessons a year.

Cover supervisors should only cover short term. Short term is normally 3 continuous days for one teacher. So for example, you should only see the same groups for a maximum of 3 times before a supply teacher is called in. This makes sense, if you were a parent, how would you feel if your child was being taught by a non-subject specific, non-qualified teacher? Therefore supply teachers have to be called in, after the 3 days of absence.

You should never be used to plan any lessons or mark any work. Your main role is to issue the work to pupils given to you by a teacher, ensure that pupils remain safe while in your care and follow the school rules. In other words, babysitting. In some lessons it can be seen like this, however it doesn't often happen. As I have mentioned before, pupils will play up, and when not enough work has been left – this is where you have to think on your feet, and you really work for your wage.

> To do. Check your job description and compare it to one located on the internet. They won't be identical, but the duties should be similar. It's easy to be taken for granted

...tion

...gs for the word differentiation. The first ...g horrible and over complicated in ... - and luckily not what we are discussing here.

Differentiation in schools, is understanding the needs of the pupils and altering the work in some way to help them access the curriculum. An example of this is using coloured paper for pupils who suffer from visual stress syndrome.

Normally teachers will incorporate all sorts of differentiation into their lessons. For example, giving some of their group either harder or easier work than their peers. The reason behind it, is regardless of the pupil's ability, they should all take away something from the lesson. This is very much a tailored way of teaching, and very much encouraged by Ofsted.

However, when it comes to writing cover lessons (very often, not by their regular teacher) – you'll be lucky to get enough work for the whole lesson. Normally within this lesson, it will be a "one size fits all". Where all the pupils will have to do all the tasks. Obviously this puts you, and the pupils at a distinct disadvantage. Although, it doesn't stop you from differentiating the work. As cover supervisors – we have to differentiate by outcome. This just means that you allow some pupils to complete some of the work, others to finish most of the tasks, while pushing a few to do an additional task or 2.

> This is something that you may do all the time without knowing. It's nice to put a name to "that thing"

Disrespectfulness

As an authoritative figure stood at the front of the class, it would be nice to receive some respect from those rosy cheek "dumplings" sat in front of you. How wrong can you be?

In a time gone by, yes children did respect their elders, and should be seen and not heard… However times have moved on considerably. In the curriculum now, children are encouraged to have an opinion and in most cases are not scared of sharing it.

Let's be realistic, respect needs time to be earned. Their regular teacher has spent a lot of lesson time, winning them over and securing their respect and forming boundaries to work within.

As a cover supervisor, we only have an hour, and some miracles can take a little longer than that to happen. In short, you have to give respect to earn it. This, no matter how badly behaved the pupils are, always treat them with dignity. Once you take away their self-respect, and possibly publicly embarrassed them to prove a point (yes, I've seen this happen!) You also remove the opportunity of exchanging respect. The pupil's self-respect is replaced by remorse, the feeling of hatred towards you, and in some cases have the relentless need to get one up on you.

In some cases their frustrated that their regular teacher is absent, and takes it out on you. It's not personal. This, can also be a work avoidance strategy.

| Respect has to be earned – be persistent |

Demonstrate

Don't be fooled in believing that only teachers can demonstrate things to pupils. As an adult within school we all have a responsibility to show and demonstrate how to behave in the adult world. In addition to their academic studies, pupils will develop social and emotional skills that they can take forward into their working life.

So for example, if a pupil requires the toilet, I try to discourage them by telling the pupil that when they start work they may not be lucky enough to be able to go when they want, and that they should get into good habits while at school.

Some pupils may come from families that have a history of unemployment. With these pupils, you have to explain the skills and discipline needed to be able to keep a job. Explaining why it's important to arrive to lesson on time, can be easily transferred to working life, if you're late to work you may lose your job.

I've had situations where colleagues have spoken to me rather rudely (an instance was, a member of staff expected the regular teacher to be teaching – and blamed me for her absence) in front of the class that I was covering. I had to deal with this in a professional way, even though the pupils were saying they'd slap her. I had to explain that as an adult, violence is not the answer.

> Consider how you behave, as you will be demonstrating either good or bad behaviour to pupils

Do's

These may be obvious, but it's nice to be reminded of them

- ✓ Try to arrive to lesson on time
- ✓ Smile, show them you want to be there
- ✓ Stick to the lesson plan
- ✓ Ask for help if you need it
- ✓ Encourage hands up when asking questions
- ✓ Stick to your guns
- ✓ Be clear and concise when explaining the task
- ✓ Leave feedback for the teacher
- ✓ If you say you'll do it – then do it
- ✓ Be yourself
- ✓ Enjoy yourself
- ✓ Learn from your mistakes
- ✓ Observe other cover supervisors and teachers
- ✓ Report all child protection concerns
- ✓ Do the register accurately
- ✓ Check your breath and were deodorant
- ✓ Remain calm

Don'ts

Hopefully these should be apparent...

× Be negative

× Take your temper out on the current class, because of the previous one

× Pick your nose, yawn, itch your bottom in class

× Swear (Even mild words such as hell, crap and bloody)

× Allow bad behaviour to continue

× Bully, be rude or ill-mannered to any one at school

× Try to be the pupil's friend or mate

× Waffle

× Leave the classroom in a mess

× Take personal expensive items in to the classroom

× Think you know it all

× Bottle up a problem or frustration

× Eat or drink in a classroom

× Touch children at all – not even a pat on the back

× Let a pupil out of class without a note

× Shout unnecessarily

× Leave the classroom when covering

Dress Code

Within a school, you can normally guess what particular teachers teach. For example PE staff will typically were tracksuits, food technology staff may wear aprons, and science teachers will have white lab coats.

My point is these teachers know what lessons they are taking, and can dress appropriately. As a cover supervisor, you won't know what you're doing until you've picked up your paper work at the start of the day. This can course many problems.

Keep within the dress code for the school. The chances are, the dress code is going to be smart. But additionally take your coat – in case you're doing PE in winter, and then if possible were layers as you may be in that one classroom that is always warm and feels like an oven. Going from one extreme to another is the norm for a cover supervisor.

What you wear has to be comfortable (and professional) – so no slippers or onesies. You will be on your feet for most of the day, so no high heels shoes, sorry ladies.

Some schools have a dress down day (where you donate a small amount of money to a charity) – think carefully what you wear. You're favourite t-shirt with the F word on it? Some staff choose to remain in the normal attire, it takes out the stress of what to wear. Additionally you'll still have to perform your normal daily duties of being a cover supervisor. Besides, why spoil your civvies?

If in doubt – keep it simple

During the Lesson

Once the lesson has started, and the pupils know what they're doing – don't relax. Throughout the lesson, you will have pupils who believe that if they have a pen in their hand that will satisfy you. Pupils have to believe that work still has to be done even though their regular teacher is away.

Circulate! Float! Go around the classroom and keep going around. The purpose of this is to ensure that the pupils continue to work. Some pupils will not ask for help, but you may notice that one pupil isn't making as much progress as their peers. If you ask them if their ok, you're making the first move - you're braking the ice. This is all it could take.

Additionally, floating around allows you to talk to pupils and to get to know them. Taking time out, and talking to them about their hobbies brakes down that barrier and builds up a professional relationship. This is useful, when you see them again – the pupil knows that you're "ok", and will do what you ask of them. This is all about getting them on your side.

In the past I have even had one pupil stick up for me, telling another pupil "to shut it – she's ok". The male pupil wanted to play up, because their regular teacher was absent. In this situation, I had covered a German lesson, where she was in and we had a chat about the watch she was wearing. A lot of cover supervisors overlook the importance of circulating, but it is vital.

> By walking around the class room, makes you approachable and can keep an eye on potential problems

EAL Pupils

EAL stands for English as an Additional Language. This cohort of pupils are relatively new. Yes, they have special needs, in the aspect that they are bright and intelligent (in most cases) but merely cannot access the lessons because of the lack of English.

With their normal teacher, they will be given key words that have been translated and have worksheets that are set up to help them (differentiation). With a cover lesson, don't expect any of that. If you do get it, you have done well.

Depending on the length of time these pupils have been in England, will determine how much assistance they require. Some pupils may need an odd word explaining, where other pupils will have to sit next to another pupil who can help them extensively. In some lessons you will have a teaching Assistant who is assigned to the group. These are invaluable – use them to help you. They know the class well, where their up to and where they sit. Some pupils may have a dictionary or a tablet like device to use to help translate English words in to their home language, encourage them to use it.

If within a lesson, you get the group to read, never force EAL pupils to read, especially if it's a mixed group of pupils. If they volunteer, then that is brilliant. That should be heavily praised.

| EAL pupils are not stupid or deaf. So there is no reason to talk loudly or slowly. Talk to them normally |

End of the lesson

This is one of the most important parts of the lesson. Allow enough time so that the pupils have time to tidy up. If they are not let out on time to go to another lesson – they will be late and will get into trouble.

Some lessons like art, where there can be a lot to put away, start to tidy up a little earlier – say 7 minutes before the bell. If it's PE, they will have to change, so allow 10 minutes.

In an academic lesson, such as English, 5 minutes is enough. Grab their attention, by saying something like "Pens down, eyes this way" then, allow 30 seconds for take up time. Wait for quiet, then tell them where you want them to place their books, and other equipment, followed by explaining how they should show you that their ready to go. I like to see pupils standing behind their chairs. This allows me to see if all tables are clear of clutter and are tidy. Don't be scared of pointing things out, and asking them to tidy it up. Once they are stood waiting for the bell to go, let them know how pleased you were with their behaviour – for example. I do this because it means they leave on a positive. When I take their lesson again, they'll remember it.

If you don't ensure the room is left tidy, either you will have to do it, or you'll leave it in a mess for the next lesson. How would you feel if you had to work in a messy environment?

When leaving a classroom, ask yourself would you be happy covering in here? If yes – you've done a good job

Etiquette

This may seem at little strange to have in here, but I do feel that it's an important thing to include. Classroom etiquette works on many levels.

When you enter a classroom, you expect the classroom to be tidy, where you can find the class books easily and that the cover work is sat on the desk ready for you to read. There is nothing worse than going in to a classroom, where the desk is a bomb site. Ok, there is nothing you can do if the regular teacher has left it this way. Although, there is a possibility that you may be in the same classroom for up to 3 days (the maximum time a cover supervisor is allowed to cover one teacher) you'll want to keep the room organized.

Additionally if you're in the same classroom all day, let the teacher in the next classroom know your covering. They might even tell you the classes to be mindful of. Sometimes they may even pop their head in, throughout the day to see if you're ok. This helps because if feels like you're not flying solo.

Once you have covered a class, try to leave some form of feedback to the teacher. This will help them to pick up where you left off. The class may have done not as much, or more then what was planned for. The teacher needs to know this for their next lesson. Plus letting them know who caused you problems, these can be dealt with accordingly.

> In short, treat people and the rooms you're in with some decorum. You'll get respected for it, and looked after better in the future

Evacuation Procedures

It sounds posh, but merely covers everything from a fire drill to possible threats of terrorist attacks. It is vital to know what to do and how to go about it.

In every lesson you cover you must do the register in the first few minutes. This is essential, because this is the document that is used as a comparison with the second register that is completed in the playground after the evacuation. It allows the admin staff to see if every pupil is present. If there not, then they know who they are looking for.

When the alarm sounds, calmly ask the pupils to leave the room and go to the nearest exit. Ensure that every one is out, do not lock the door. The evacuation manager will need to check every room, unlocking each door will cost time and possibly lives. Once outside "check in" with the cover manager, they will tick you off their staff register. You may have to complete another pupil register. Once completed, hand it into the designated member of staff.

Until you are told to move – encourage your group of pupils to stand in a straight line, as quiet as possible. If it isn't a drill, wait until you are told what to do. You must be cooperative in these situations as there will be a lot of confusion.

Do not panic – this will alarm your pupils. Remain calm, it will help to reassure scared pupils especially if it isn't a drill

Examinations

From time to time, you will be asked to invigilate examinations. This is usually conducted in the hall. There will be many staff doing the same thing. Your role will be to ensure that the pupils have everything they need so that they can complete the exam. You may have to fetch a pen or pencil as they are not allowed to move once they have been seated.

If you know in advance that you're invigilating in the exam, think ahead. Wear shoes that don't make a noise when you walk, rubber soles are best. It can be off putting hearing the click of a shoe when you need to concentrate. Equally, if you have jewellery that jangles when you move, consider removing it before you enter the room.

You can read out the question if a pupil asks, but you cannot explain what it means. The exam is testing their understanding of the subject, not testing their reading skills (unless it's a reading test).

Which brings us nicely on to pupils with learning difficulties – such as dyslexia. Of course these are highly intelligent pupils. These pupils are sometimes placed in a separate room, where their TA (who will read out the questions ONLY) will not put off other pupils in the exam.

Other pupils may need a scriber, somebody to write for them. They may have a broken arm for example – that prevents them from writing. The scriber has no input, they just write what they have been told to.

Shhh! Think quiet, be seen and not herd when in exams

Extension Exercises

Don't worry – you won't get out of breath, or grow an extra inch with this. This is the name given to an extra task, for when the pupils have finished the main body of work and it's not the end of the lesson yet.

Chances are, the lesson plan will have been quickly written, where no thought to the content or any extra tasks has been given. This is why it's important to be prepared.

Sometimes it may satisfy the pupils to just draw a "poster" that recaps the content of the lesson. This can motivate other pupils to finish their work, so that they can draw! However for higher ability pupils, this isn't good enough - they'll complain. The extension task should be fun, they've completed all the work, and it should be seen as a treat.

Other extension ideas can be for the pupils to write a blog or a Facebook page on the topic. This encourages them to be imaginative and embeds what they have learnt. I have a blank Facebook template that I display on the board. The pupils can use that for a template. This is easy enough to do.

I'd suggest that you search for similar tasks that take next to no time to prepare and uses only basic resources. A "think board" is another idea, where the pupil divides their page into 4. They have to ask a question, draw a diagram, write a short paragraph on the topic and write down something that they don't understand about the subject. One task, per box.

| Be prepared and plan ahead |

Facial Expressions

Getting your facial expressions right can be difficult. It can make all the difference, as pupils will know whether to take you seriously or not, when telling them off, or even to let them know they are doing a good job.

For instance if you need to warn or tell off a pupil, you cannot do it when your smiling. This is a mixed message, the pupil will not take you seriously, and won't take any notice of you. It is something that you will have to practice.

Additionally, "that look" can save you from shouting. It can be used when "those girls" are talking when you are. To use it, simply stop what you're saying (in mid-sentence) and look straight at the girls. Pause as long as it takes the girls to stop talking. The shear embarrassment is enough for them not to do it again, and is a warning for other pupils not to do it at all. "The look" that you give is vital for this to work. It has to have an element of anger and frustration, folding your arms also helps with this.

With that in mind we can turn the tables, and learn to read the pupils. This can take time, but after a little time and experience you'll know if a pupil is lying or chewing gum when they say they're not. When you can do it, it really worries them, because they think your reading their mind. It's quite funny actually – but you can't laugh (well at least not at that point).

I have only skimmed the surface of facial expressions, once again talk to people and use the internet to learn more in greater detail about this

Feedback

It is only courtesy to give feedback to the teacher about the lesson that they have missed. If they have taken time to prepare a cover lesson, it's only polite to let them know how it went.

The information that is required includes how much work the majority (not all will complete everything) of the class have done, any problems that you have encountered that prevented you from following the lesson plan. Additionally you should also mention a couple of pupils who were really good in the lesson – they could have completed all the work, or helped you to find the books. Equally you should also mention pupils who didn't behave, those who refused to do the work or had to be moved room.

Other pieces of information that you could include is any extension excises that you had to do – that wasn't on the plan. This will politely tell the teacher that not enough, or good enough work was set. If the teacher has any integrity they will take the feedback on board and improve their practice for next time.

At the end of the lesson, it is also a good idea to let the class know how you think they have done. By saying something like, "Most of you have done really well, I'll pass it on to Mr Palmer…"

As much as the lesson plan was written badly, and you'd like to tell the teacher exactly what you think of it. Don't. Be the professional one, and rise above it

Fighting Fires

Realistically you may be one of many cover supervisors that the class has seen in a very short time. Being a teacher is very stressful, where pupils are now seen as commodities. Teachers have to lift pupil's national curriculum levels up by 3 sub levels in a year, and that's every pupil - including the low ability and the naughtiest. Of course the temptation, is to remove that one naughty pupil, to allow the others to learn. In this instance, that one naughty pupil isn't learning when he has been removed from the classroom. Do teachers (and the other pupils) just put up with that naughty pupil, because "every child matters"?

Luckily cover supervisors, don't have that pressure of being accountable for results. But the pressure that we have is to convince the pupils to complete the work when either they don't want to, or the work set has not been thought through and is as dull as ditch water.

Pupils are not stupid, they know what's going on. They also know when their being neglected by their regular teacher, or that department. You are the one that they will have a go at, not because it's personal – but they want to learn and are not being given the chance to be taught. In this case, listen to them, and tell them that you will pass on their concerns – and do it. They will feel better that somebody has listened to them, and taken notice of them.

> Some classes will fall unlucky and end up with "that teacher", who is always off. Just be sympathetic to the pupils, and listen to their needs, without crossing that professional line

First Impressions

Please, I beg of you, don't act like an idiot! Don't let the power go to your head, or feel that you should behave like a games show host, or be desperate enough to act like their mate during lessons.

When covering a class for the first time, for instance a year 7 group in September. Introduce yourself to them, explain your classroom rules and clarify that you're in close contact with their teacher. Try to keep the rules to a minimum, my rules are

- No talking while I am, because its rude
- Hands up, if you want my attention
- Respect the room, and everyone and everything in it

As you notice, my rules are simple and not over complicated. When the pupils know that your straight talking and assertive, and that you stick to your rules – they'll appreciate it. Once you have established a set of rules, if the pupils meet you again, they'll know what to expect. And with this, it will get easier.

Some groups you'll see again and again, and your heart will sink when they appear on your daily time table. They don't like you, and you don't like them. With these groups, you have to cover it, that's what your there for. My advice is be professional, and get on with it – and stick to your rules. And remember it's only an hour.

> Set good standards and high expectations, as difficult as it is, it will pay off in the future

Flexibility

With this, I'm not suggesting that you should be a contortionist by any means. But do accept that what lessons (and frees) that you are given at the start of the day – may not be what you actually do.

During the day, teachers may have to go home because they've become too ill to teach, so their lessons will need covering, or that the teacher you were going to cover- their meeting has been cancelled. The point is, whatever your time table looks like at 8.30, may not resemble the day that you've actually done.

Each school will have their own method of letting you know that your lessons have changed. For example the cover manager may come and find you to let you know, and replace your cover list with a fresh one with the alterations on. While other schools prefer you to have your mobile phone at hand so that they can contact you and notify you of the changes.

Whichever way you are told that your lessons have altered, accept them – even though you had plans to phone home about some of the pupils in your free. To be honest, the schools priority is to ensure that all pupils are at least being supervised, it's a safeguarding issue. As cover supervisors, we have to grab our free lessons as, and when we get them.

Because we never know what our day has in store for us, try and keep a breast with admin, don't rely on waiting for that free – it may be taken off of you. When you get your free – use it well

Form Time

Yes, you will be asked to cover form time. You'll need to know which day of the week the group's assembly occurs. On assembly days do the register first - this is essential. Make sure that the pupils are looking smart, with ties done properly and shirts are tucked in. Then escort them down to assembly, trying to encourage them to be quiet when walking through school. When in assembly, follow the other staff, some schools like the staff to stand at the sides, while others prefer staff to sit amongst the pupils.

If it isn't assembly, then the class will remain in their form room. Typically this is a busy time of the day, it's where notices are given out, and admin tasks are conducted. As a cover supervisor, it's difficult to pick up from the day before. Pupils may give you money for a trip or hand in consent forms. If you belong to the school, you'll know where these should go. If you're from an agency send them down to the reception (with a note). The reception will be able to deal with these pupils.

Form time usually lasts for about 20 minutes. It is very rare to receive a lesson plan for this time (although you should do). During this time, circulate and ensure that all pupils have correct uniform, planners and equipment to write with. If you have access to the internet, and the interactive white board, put a news channel on. Get them to watch the news.

Treat form time like a lesson. Think about what you're going to do, may be think of doing simple literacy games such as hangman on the white board

Free Lessons

From time to time you will get a free lesson when you're not needed to cover. With these you can have one of two attitudes. Time for a brew in the staff room? Or actually do something, such as feedback to teachers, phone home to parents or search for activities or ideas that will help you in your lessons.

I'm not one to criticise you for having a brew, especially if you've had a rotten class beforehand. However, if you do it too often, it will be frown upon.

On a free lesson, use it wisely because you never know when the next one will be. Think of it as getting ahead, rather than catching up. During these lessons, I like to find new ideas, so that I can use them when either the work has run out, or no work has been set. The only rules that I have, is that it must be able to be adapted to most subjects, and that it doesn't take any time at all to set up or use resources that cannot be found in a normal classroom. This helps me feel in control. If you work in a team of cover supervisors, share what you have found. Don't be scared of going on websites that are aimed at teachers. On frees, you can support teaching staff, and take notice of the activities that they use, they might give you an idea that you could use in your lessons.

Whatever you decide to do, let the cover manager know what you're doing, and where they can find you – just in case

Further Reading

This is something I strongly suggest you do either if you're happy to remain as a cover supervisor, or if you want to progress further. This list below is a mixture of books aimed at both teaching assistants and teachers, they cover all areas of experience and expertise.

- Level 3 Diploma Supporting Teaching and Learning in Schools, *Primary*, Candidate Handbook, by Ms Louise Burnham, Mrs Brenda Baker
- Level 3 Diploma Supporting Teaching and Learning in Schools, *Secondary*, Candidate Handbook: The Teaching Assistant's Handbook, by Ms Louise Burnham, Mrs Brenda Baker
- Teaching Today A Practical Guide Fourth Edition, by Geoff Petty
- Evidence-Based Teaching A Practical Approach Second Edition, by Geoff Petty
- Teacher's Toolkit: Raise Classroom Achievement with Strategies for Every Learner, by Paul Ginnis
- 100 Ideas for Supply Teachers, by Julia Murphy
- Classroom Behaviour: A Practical Guide to Effective Teaching, Behaviour Management and Colleague Support, by Bill Rogers

> Don't worry, I'm not saying you should (but you could) read all of these books, but it will definitely benefit you and your understanding of school, pupils and your practice

Fun

This page comes with a warning!

Yes, you and the class should have fun. Learning should be enjoyable but it can soon become out of control, and it can become uncontrollable extremely quickly.

This is where you are stuck between a rock and a hard place. You still have to follow the lesson plan, but you also have to make it interesting to motivate the pupils so that they work. It can be difficult doing this within the boundaries of the lesson.

The solution behind this problem, is your personality! You can put a spin on that particular topic, as you have got life experiences that you can talk about and bring that topic to life. Additionally, the pupils, may prefer you to their regular teacher and hang off every word that you say.

Alternatively, if it's an older class compromise with them. Tell them that if they are working and working quietly you will put the radio on. Providing that you have access to the internet and the interactive white board has speakers. I will suggest strongly that you choose a radio station, not a site that allows you to choose each song. Pupils will then start to squabble about what to play next (and it also ties you to the computer, as you need to type in each song title), and the other suggestion is to keep the music on the quiet- this means they have to be quiet to listen to it.

> Having fun is always good, but you have to work extra hard to maintain order. Pupils do tend to get carried away, and it can soon become fairly noisy and disruptive

Gender

This is where "pupils" are turned back into children, and we discover that girls and boys are extremely different. Their rate of emotional, developmental, and intelligence develops at different speeds. For example girls tend to mature earlier than boys (generally speaking), and will consider that some of the boys in the class are "sad and pathetic".

Academically, boys find maths, physics and sport easier than girls. On the other hand girls enjoy English, history and RE better. Of course this is extremely stereotypical, and you'll come across exceptions to this rule. But with this in mind, you have to be aware that girls will struggle with some subjects, while being a high flyer in others, this is exactly the same with boys.

As a cover supervisor, you can use this information, by understanding that you'll have to motivate one gender more than the other in certain subjects. There is no point saying "but you worked well in ... (whatever the subject), how come you're not working at the same pace now?" Pupils are just like us, there are things we like to do more than other things, and therefore put more effort in to the things we like. Pupils are just the same.

When you are addressing the group, avoid using words such as guys. This can be seen as a masculine word, and can offend the girls

Gifted & Talented (G&T)

Chances are, you will not know who these pupils are. The reason is simple. With some lessons, you might only get a sentence or two to explain what the absent teacher wants the class to do. As I have mentioned earlier in this book, differentiation should be set to accommodate all pupils with additional needs – including those who are G&T.

G&T pupils are an odd bunch of pupils. They can be gifted or talented in a certain subject - such as sport for example but haven't a clue when it comes to science.

As like with any cohort of pupils, there should be a register of these pupils. The information on this register will detail who they are, what their gift or talent is, and any intervention that the school is doing to push them. The information on this register should be available to all staff.

It may be obvious that you have a G&T pupil in your class, when they have completed all the work, in super quick time. Giving these pupils a poster to draw will not satisfy them. They like to be challenged, and just saying "turn to the next page in the text book" is a bad idea. That might be the next lesson. Ask these pupils to write in their words, "what would happen if…" and link it to the lesson.

Research extension activities for these high ability pupils, tasks that can be used in a number of subjects are going to be beneficial. Additionally, they can also be used for other earlier finishers

Ground Rules

Ground rules are so important for a cover supervisor. On your first meeting of any class, it is important to set them out, so the pupils know what you expect of them.

Pupils like consistency and routine, when their regular teacher is absent – bang goes their routine. As a cover supervisor, we have to ensure that the pupils still maintain some sense of boundaries, it provides a sense of security. And this is where the ground rules come in.

Your ground rules are going to be personal to you, and they are going to be the ones that you use in all the subjects that you cover. The purpose of this, is that when pupils see you, (regardless of the subject) they know what you expect of them. Your rules must be few in number, and try to remain concise. This is a list of my rules:

- No talking while I am, because it's rude
- Hands up, if you want my attention
- Respect the room, and everyone and everything in it

Always stick to your rules, if you can't - how do you expect the pupils to? Don't continue talking over pupils, never answer to a pupil shouting out, and always respect everyone and everything. At times this may be difficult, but it will be worth it in the end.

| Remember – lead by example |

High Expectations

This is another topic that is as much for you as it is for the pupils in front of you. Ok, it's a fact that you're not a teacher, but you're doing a job that not many people would fancy doing. At times the role can be very demanding, just because you're not a teacher, why shouldn't you ask for high expectations, of yourself, and the pupils that you meet?

You'll hear it enough times, from the pupils "you're not our proper teacher…"When you hear that, remind yourself that this is merely an excuse not to work or behave for you. At the end of the day, you do not go to work, for people (or pupils in our case) to talk to us like we are worth nothing.

Have some self-respect, believe that you do deserve pupils to be at least civil to you. You are an adult, not one of them. Once you accept this, it is easier to enforce it. I personally do not accept any rudeness, swearing or bullying. After a few lessons with me, the pupils that I meet eventually know this. In practice, this means that any pupil I see or hear, going against my rules, I deal with immediately. My expectations are nothing new or different but they are general guidelines that pupils should be following any way. But sometimes pupils need reminding that it isn't just teachers that expect good behaviour. The idea is that you need to be consistent with them.

Give yourself a break, it's a tough job as a cover supervisor, use this to your own advantage. Demand high expectations, regardless of your qualifications (or lack of them).

Holidays

Contrary to belief, whoever you work for (either based in one school or an agency) unlike teachers you do not get paid for all 13 weeks of school holidays.

If you are based in one school you will work on a pro-rata. This means you only get paid for the actual 39 weeks (this includes 5 training days') that you work plus 5 weeks for statutory holiday pay. Your salary is then divided by 12 (months) and the total is what you get paid every month.

For example

| £ Per hour | x | No Hours per week | X | 44 work weeks | = | salary | ÷ | 12 month | = | Total wage |

If you work for an agency, it's simple no work no wage. This is where you either have to be good with money and manage the money you have well, or getting a second job either at the weekend or holidays.

On a lighter note, if you work near your school be very careful in what you do, during holiday time. The chances are, you will be seen by a pupil! If you don't want pupils seeing you in a compromising situation then don't do it there. But you're not safe anywhere, I've even bumped in to pupils (and their parents) abroad.

Appreciate the time off, as a cover supervisor – you've deserve it

Homework

On the lesson plan, the teacher may mention that homework is due in. And of course, we all know the response of the pupils. It will be a selection of excuses from my dog, Sprocket ate it, and to I didn't think we had to hand it in today... When you are writing your feedback – don't forget to mention that you prompted them regarding homework but not many pupils handed it in. This covers you, and it high lights which pupils have/haven't done the homework.

If you're lucky enough to have a lesson plan that has been written well, it may ask you to even handout homework. In this case, allow enough time to explain what the task is, as well as tidying up. When giving feedback, make a note of the pupils who were absent and didn't receive it. The teacher can work out through looking at the handed in homework and your list, the pupils who are not on either list are the ones who haven't done the homework.

Some pupils will blame anyone but themselves for avoiding doing homework. Of course, they will believe that this will work because they won't know that you've left feedback regarding this.

Again, this backs up many concepts mentioned in this book. Pupils will eventually realise that they can't "win" if you're doing your job right.

If you want to become better at this role, or progress in your career, you'll have to do some homework yourself. Read, research or study

Ice Breakers

Having a selection of ice breakers can be useful. They can be given to the group, to occupy them until you have logged on to the PC, and read (and absorbed) the cover lesson, located the books needed, or in some cases figure out what to do when you know the cover work is far from good.

A good ice breaker should be one that you can introduce to the group and is simple enough for them to do it, without being hassled too much from them while you get sorted.

A good example of this is asking the group to go through the alphabet and assigning a word to each letter. So in an English lesson, A = alliteration, B = balanced sentence, C = chiasmus and so on. As you can imagine this can be used in any subject.

Finding good ice breakers can be time consuming, but it might be something you may want to do in those elusive free lessons. When searching on the internet, search for classroom starters, and ice breakers. Some ideas are going to be better than others, or you may want to alter some ideas to fit how you use it. Teachers do this all the time. They find an idea, and tweak it to fit their lessons.

In some lessons you may only be covering for part of it, so a small activity – such as an ice breaker may just do the trick.

> Don't be put off by looking at sites that have been designed for teachers. You are replacing the teacher when you're covering – so why shouldn't you use the same resources?

Illness

Yes, without illness, most cover supervisors would be out of a job. Nevertheless, teachers who are absent from school due to illness, do not have to set work! Now, this explains a lot, doesn't it?

A lot of teachers who are passionate and bothered about their classes will set work – if they physically can. Some teachers will email in their work. The head of department or the cover manager will print it off ready for you. Although some teachers, may phone in and explain the cover work. Doing it this way is like playing Chinese whispers. Whoever answers the phone, may be doing something else at the time. They'll take the message, but it'll be in note form. Phoning in allows for mistakes to happen, and the lesson plan is more likely to be brief.

Although – if a teacher is ill, they do not have to set the work. This is within their terms and conditions as a teacher. If no work has been set, then it's down to the head of department to guess where each of their classes are up to, and then try to set work without knowing the pupils in the class. This is really where our problems stem from.

And, this is the point of this book. Illness happens, bad lesson plans will be written and classes will misbehave. Please do not be under any illusion that these things will get better. They won't! But what will improve is how you deal with these problems.

> If you have to phone in, because you're ill – make sure you know the procedure before you need to use it

Inclusion

Inclusion is a term that is used a lot in and around school. In its simplest form, it means that all pupils must be included in all activities at school. It sounds simple, but when you look closer it starts to get complicated. Regarding academic subjects, pupils with learning difficulties have to have the same opportunities of learning as everyone else. This is why teachers should use differentiation. Just because a pupil has dyslexia – this does not mean that they should be at a disadvantage when learning about volcanos in geography for example. The teacher has to help that pupil to be able to access the information.

On a practical note, inclusion applies to pupils who have extra physical requirements. Most newly built schools have lifts, these allow pupils to attend lessons that are on the second or third floor despite being in a wheelchair.

This also infringes on equality and diversity. This is a massive subject, I cannot do it justice here. So in a nutshell, it is all about making things fair and not discriminating against things such as gender, religion, age or skin colour. This is everywhere from schools to employment. Within school, we have to accept and celebrate differences. Hopefully this will prevent any type of discrimination.

Use this information in the classroom by understanding that no matter how hard some pupils try – they just can't do the work. If this happens, alter the work so that they can. You are being inclusive – even when the lesson plan wasn't

Independent Learning

This is where pupils take control of their learning, find out things for themselves without having to ask for help. When covering a lesson, sometimes you'll be given a text book, and a page number. With most text books, you have to read the page and answer the questions linked with the page. All the answers are in the text. When I explain the task, I'll say turn to page 47 (for example), the pupils need to read the text and answer the questions.

In reality the pupils will bypass the text and go straight to the questions, and then struggle to answer them. They'll do this, to try and complete the work sooner, so that they can have a natter. About 10 minutes in, up goes their hands, "Miss, miss I need help..." When covering, my reply is "Well did you read the text?" This helps to hide the fact, that I have no idea what they're going on about because I haven't read it either, as I only saw the book for the first time 15 minutes ago. Additionally, this encourages them to read the text.

A lot of pupils do not know how to research a question, some books have an end of unit page, where questions are asked, and the pupil should look at a number of pages to locate the answers. This is a skill that you can pass on, show them how to use the index and glossary of a book. It is surprising how many pupils do not know how to use them.

Independent learning is a skill that has to be taught, something that quite often the teacher over looks

Interpersonal Skills

As a cover supervisor, your interpersonal skills are vital to be successful. Yes, you'll have some pretty grotty classes, where no work has been set and the behaviour of the pupils is in short, dreadful. If you find that a lot of lessons either have no work set, or the work is substandard, it may be worth highlighting this to senior management. Although to be taken seriously, make a note of lessons that you've covered, and bring what work has been left (both good and bad examples). With this evidence hopefully you will be taken seriously. Additionally, if you can discuss a possible solution to the problem, this will avoid the senior management trying to tackle a problem that they didn't know existed, with a solution that realistically just wouldn't work in the classroom, and may cause even more problems in the long run.

Additionally, having good people skills can be useful in the classroom. For example, trying to encourage pupils to work, when they don't want to. As frustrating as it is, you can't lose it, because it will be counterproductive. Understanding how to get the best results, without kicking up a fuss is a good skill to have. It may not come over night, you will have to work at it, but it is worth working at.

Watch other people, and their interpersonal skills. Obviously some will be better than others, watch and learn

Job Description

From school to school, the job description will differ. But primarily the job description will state that you will deliver lessons in the absence of the regular teacher, sometimes at short notice. Another point that most job descriptions will include is that you will manage the behaviour of the pupils in accordance to the school behaviour policy. These are the main aspects of the cover supervisor job description, but each job description will have many more points. Their fore it is important to read it and know exactly what the school wants you to do.

I'd like to draw your attention to what you are not supposed to do. As a cover supervisor, you should not be expected to plan work, mark work or cover lessons longer than 3 consecutive days for one teacher. Their strict guidelines to what you can and can't do. If your school asks you to do something that I have listed, or something that you do not think is right. Contact your union representative, and talk to them, don't forget to take your job description.

Additionally, right at the bottom of most job descriptions will be a statement that will say you'll have to do other duties, if the school requests them. This covers the school if they have forgotten something. This is a normal statement on most job descriptions now a days. Other duties could include attending a parents evening, or handing out uniform at the start of the year.

If you haven't done so already, read your job description. If there is something on that you don't understand or agree with – check it out with Human Resources and your union

Key Stage

This is a term that is banded around a lot at school, I thought it was useful to include it, as it may help you progress in your career. There are 6 stages from 0 to 5. Pupils go from one stage to another as they progress through the education system. It is not based on ability – but age. Below is a table showing the correlation of key stage and pupil age.

Key Stage	Pupil Age	School Year	School type
0	3-5		Nursery
1	5-7	1 & 2	Primary
2	7-11	3, 4, 5 &6	Primary
3	11-14	7, 8 & 9	Secondary
4	14-16	10 & 11	Secondary
5	16-18	12 & 13	College

Just to mess around with your head, another term that has crept in is "age, not stage". Some schools, have taken this idea on where they believe that if a pupil has the ability to move up, then let them move up early. The idea is that if the pupil is bright enough, the key stage system prevents them from progressing.

To a cover supervisor this would look like: All pupils in one class would not all belong to the same year group. In regards of completing the register, the pupils would be timetabled for that lesson, so all the pupils would be on the same register.

Keys

Yes you will need keys. All classrooms should be locked when they're not in use. Some classrooms may have a different key to other rooms. With this in mind you may end up with a number of keys to open a selection of rooms.

I remember when I first started trying to explain to "the key master" (the bloke who had always worked in an office and had no idea what I did.) "… but no other staff has so many keys", I very politely explained again and I eventually got the keys.

Yes, you may face some resistance when asking for keys, but keep at it. Having a key that opens the door, allows your class to start on time, rather than begging other staff to open the door for you.

When you have your set of keys, you have responsibility. You cannot leave them anywhere, or lose them. I have a key ring that clips on to my belt. Here, the keys are at a nice height, where I can get them easily. When you've to dash from one room to another, its little things like that, which save time. If you have many keys that look the same, put a coloured topper on them. For example if the green corridor have one key, place a green topper on it. And likewise for the red corridor, and another for the English block. This means you can identify them easily at a glance.

Don't lose your keys – not even in the loo!

Lateness

There is two sides to this topic, it affects both you and the pupils. Sometimes it is unavoidable not being on time, reasons include; you'll either have to deal with something from the previous class, you get stopped on the corridor by a teacher or you've had to dash from one side of the school to the other. These are valid reasons for not being on time. In these cases, demonstrate how to behave when you're late to the pupils who are waiting. Apologise to the pupils for being late, and then move swiftly on to the start of the lesson.

Similarly some pupils will be late to your lesson. Some of them will have a legitimate reason for being late – such as they have had an instrument lesson (sometimes they work out of sync with normal lesson times), or they have had some form of intervention with another member of staff. For genuine reasons the pupil will have a note to explain their lateness.

However on the other hand, some pupils will see that they have a "supply" and decide to go to the toilet. They do this, because they believe that the consequences will not stand because the regular teacher isn't present. And, rather worryingly, they devalue these lessons because the work set, isn't what they have been doing in recent lessons, and that it's just been set to "keep them occupied". When these pupils do eventually come in, don't make a fuss of them. Mark them late on the register, then ask for their reason, when the class is on task.

> Don't make a fuss, this only waste time. Some pupils want you to make a fuss – it cuts down their working time

Learning Difficulties

Sometimes it will be obvious that some pupils have a learning difficulty. Other times, the learning difficulty will not be as apparent. A teaching assistant may be present in the lesson, don't be scared of asking who they're supporting. If the teaching assistant is any good, they will also tell you the nature of the class, and who to keep an eye on in the lesson.

Learning difficulties are funny things. Each difficulty will have typical characteristics, but pupils will not have all the characteristics linked with that problem. This is why there are professionals who are highly qualified to recognise learning difficulties, additionally some pupils may have more than one problem, an example of this is a pupil can be diagnosed with both dyslexia and dyspraxia.

If there is a pupil with some sort of learning difficulty, do not be patronising towards them. Quite often, most of these pupils are highly intelligent. The only problem that you will encounter with these, is that the work set may not include any differentiated work for them. With this in mind, you may have to help them complete the work – but they will certainly understand the lesson content. Remember, see the pupil not the learning difficulty – the pupil will appreciate this.

Other learning difficulties include dyscalculia, dysgraphia, ADHD and autism.

> This is a massive topic, you'll benefit from talking to the SENCO, or researching this topic yourself

Learning Styles

Everybody has a preferred way of learning. There are 3 basic styles, we learn by watching, listening or by doing. There is a quiz that you can do. This will tell you, your preferred way of learning. Just search "honey and mumford learning styles questionnaire".

Pupils are exactly the same. It's worth knowing about this, because you'll understand why some pupils just don't engage with some subjects. For example some pupils don't like doing art because it relies on visual learning, but they excel in subjects such as wood work because it's a doing lesson.

If you spend any time at all in education, you'll realise that a new piece of research is released almost every week, and it replaces an older piece. If you do any research yourself on learning styles, there are many people who have studied this. It is now believed that pupils should practice all learning styles, rather than just using their preferred style. I agree with this, as it strengthens their weaker styles. In the world of work, they cannot choose, to do one task over another – you've just got to get on with it.

A good lesson plan should have elements of all the learning styles. Unfortunately a cover lesson may not include all aspects of learning styles. The outcome of this, is that some pupils will "turn off". You can try to make lessons more interesting by including a discussion perhaps

Lesson Plans

Yes, lesson plans do exist!

In an ideal world, teachers will write them on a weekly basis, they will be detailed and take into account differentiation and have the resources already – in fact good enough for a surprise Ofsted visit.

In reality, an experience teacher will know their subject and each lesson to the point of not bothering writing a lesson plan. A lot of the information that they should enter on a plan is repetitive, for example the total number of pupils, how many boys, girls, EAL and SEN are in the lesson. Some teachers tend not to bother because the only person who sees this plan is them, so why bother? This is their opinion. This is fine, unless their poorly. This is where the problems starts. If teachers are unwell, they do not have to set work. And if their sick, like anyone else, will not want to put the effort in in setting work.

For a cover supervisor, in most cases a lesson plan may consist of one line of text, for the whole lesson. This is where cover supervisors have to be prepared and have a backup of activities that they can use at a moment's notice. Additionally, lesson plans should be accompanied with a seating plan. But if you get one of these, pupils may complain that it isn't a current one. Be assertive, and insist that they sit where they should – they will not like it.

Never expect a full and complete lesson plan – you'll never be disappointed

Life Skills

Ok, in our job description, it will state that cover supervisors should not actually teach a lesson. This is why many lessons will say "continue with work from the last lesson".

With this in mind, cover supervisors can demonstrate certain skills. As I have mentioned before, pupils learn other skills other than the academic ones while at school. For instance, when covering a lesson, we still expect manners. For some pupils, this will need mentioning. Just because we are not their regular teacher, does that we need less respect?

Other skills that we can pass on are basic numeracy and literacy skills, we can still reinforce their importance. In cover lessons, I have found that some pupils find it easier to question certain issues, as their regular teacher may be offended. For example, "why do we have to do…", for some pupils this is a time avoidance method, while others genuinely want to know. In my opinion, I answer it honestly. In some subjects, pupils are not going to need that particular piece of information for life, but will need it to gain a higher grade in their GCSE's. A good grade in GCSE's demonstrates intelligence and the ability to work under pressure and the skill to recall information. This can be a great motivator for pupils who "don't see the point in doing…."

Life skills, including how you talk to people, dealing with problems and coping under pressure. You are a role model, it's down to you whether you are a good or bad one

Literacy

In most lessons, literacy skills are needed. Just because we cover lessons, we can still embed literacy. In the majority of cover lessons, pupils will be asked to "read through a text book and answer the questions". As I have mentioned previously, some pupils will bypass the reading part and go straight to the questions, where they'll then answer in a one word format.

If I have one of these types of lessons, I will let a number of pupils to read out a loud, where the rest of the class follow. I never make pupils read, I allow pupils to volunteer. Each pupil will read one paragraph before letting another take over. When the "readers" have finished reading, we (as a class) will discuss what was in the text, and I'll explain certain terms that weren't clear in the book. Going back to learning styles, doing this covers the visual and auditory learners (and in some cases kills time, when not enough work has been set).

When it comes to writing, I ensure that all pupils answer the text book questions in full and complete sentences. In secondary school, they'll know how to do them but not do it, because it saves time. Pull them up on it, and ask them to rewrite the answers correctly.

Ensure that your literacy skills are up to scratch. There is nothing more embarrassing then being pulled up on your own literacy by a pupil. The answer to this is continually read and write. Practice makes perfect

Medical Emergencies

Children are children and accidents will happen. With this in mind, we can minimise the risk. But as a cover supervisor this is not always possible. It is suggested, that before pupils enter a classroom that you should check the room before the pupils come in. This means that you make sure that wires are away neatly, and anything that is damaged is removed and reported. If you're running late to a lesson, you can't always keep pupils on the corridor while you check the room.

For problems such as nose bleeds, the pupil must be allowed to go immediately - the pupil could be bleeding heavily. Plus, on the sight of blood, other pupils can feel faint or even get excited about it.

If a pupil faints or blacks out – do not move them. Send a responsible pupil to get a first aider. Keep calm and try and prevent the other pupils from crowding around. There may be other health problems going on with the pupil that you are not aware of. If the pupil comes around, reassure them that everything is ok and wait for the first aider to come.

With headaches this could be an excuse to avoid doing any work. Let them get a drink of water, as headaches can be a symptom of dehydration. Never give any pupils any tablets, such as paracetamol.

You could ask to go on a first aid course, they range from basic training to a four day course that goes into much greater detail

Meet, greet and correct

Once again, this is all about in an ideal world. In this ideal world, all staff should stand at the classroom door and meet all the pupils who are in your lesson, welcome them into your room, and if their uniform isn't right, then ask them to put it right. In some schools, this is an expectation for teaching staff to do.

As a cover supervisor, you may have to move room, turn on the computer, locate the cover work, and find the books you need for the lesson and then have a selection of pupils asking if you're taking them for the lesson. With all this, it is impossible to meet, greet and correct.

However if your based in the same classroom all day you can meet, greet and correct. It is just a matter of being organized and setting up in the change over time, just as the regular teacher would.

These rules, such as meet, greet and correct have come from the senior leadership team. As with most rules, very little thought has been given to how cover supervisors should respond to these. Unfortunately this is how it is with cover supervisors. When the senior leadership team are reminded about cover supervisors, regarding clarification of the rules and cover supervisors - often their response is, I'll get back to you. But they never do.

In many things, cover supervisors will get over looked and forgotten about. Try to keep to the rules the best you can, but be realistic that it may not always be possible to

Meetings

Yes you might be used to cover staff who are in a meeting. If this is the case, it's a planned absence so there should be work set. If the meeting is with somebody from outside the school it may have a start and finish time that isn't in sync with the school times. For example a meeting maybe for 9 until 10, but the lesson starts at 9.15 for an hour, you will only be needed to cover for 45 minutes.

The down side to meetings, is that they may over run. You will have to stay there until that member of staff returns (if at all). If you are covering a member of staff who is also a head of year, there is every possibility that they may have a meeting with a parent. If that parent has a number of issues to air, the meeting may over run.

Some schools prefer that teachers conduct meetings outside their teaching commitments. There have been instances where certain teachers will purposely arrange meetings at a set time, so that they avoid "that class".

It's also possible that pupils have to attend meetings as well. They may be escorted back to lesson by a member of staff to explain their absence. If not they should have a note instead. Accept them into your lesson, and bring them up to speed with the task.

If you have to attend a meeting yourself, try to let your cover manager know as soon as possible. They will know that they can't use you to cover for that set time

Mobile Phones

As a general rule, no pupil should be allowed to use their phone in class. This section is really important. Mobile phones are gaining more and more functions that if used inappropriately can cost you your job!

When researching this section, I soon came across footage on the internet that a pupil had taken of a supply teacher without them knowing (the supply was dancing in the lesson). My point is within a blink of an eye (it seems like) footage can be recorded and uploaded to the internet. Mobile phones can be very dangerous.

In most schools, they don't allow pupils to have their phones out on show, let alone use them. If you see one, just remind the pupil to put it away. If the phone rings, try to encourage the pupil not to answer it and tell them to either put it on silent or turn it off. In most cases, it has just slipped their mind to sort their phone out before coming into lesson.

Tablets are another device that are becoming popular. Some schools allow them, as they can be used for learning. However the same warning is attached to these, they are still dangerous. Most tablets have a camera and can be linked to the internet easily. Some schools have given a number of cohorts (SEN, G&T and EAL) to enhance their learning. Just let them use them without making a fuss.

| Keep your eyes peeled, be quick to prompt pupils to put phones away |

Modelling

Don't worry, there are no cat walks or photographers in this section. This is about how members of staff (and I mean all staff) should be a positive role model to our pupils. Pupils watch to see how to behave and act professionally. Particularly in secondary schools, part of the emphasis is to prepare pupils for working life. Practically this means, getting them into good habits that will help them keep a job - being on time, and going to the toilet at break time are good habits.

The staff in a school could be the first group of people that pupils see working. We need to show them how to behave professionally. I have had members of staff talk to me quite badly in front of pupils. When that staff had left, pupils turned around to me and said I should have slapped them! My response to that was, that isn't how adults deal with problems, and went on to explain work isn't like the playground, where violence is the answer.

If you think about it, what other role models are available to pupils? Footballers, minor celebrities and pop bands generated from TV shows. With this calibre of role models, we have certainly got our work cut out. This is why *all* staff that work in a school need to be a good role model.

Weather your covering a class or not, you will always have to be on your best behaviour – you never know who is looking at you as an example of how to behave

Motivation

When pupils know that they have a cover supervisor their attitude alters. Normally when their regular teacher is present, they are happy to do whatever work is set for them. But when the tables are turned when they see you - some pupils tend to make the decision immediately, that whatever work you introduce to them it isn't worth doing.

There are 2 possibilities for this poor attitude. Firstly the type of work you have for them to do is not like the work they normally do with their regular teacher. It could be a practical lesson such as science, as a cover supervisor, we can't do practical's (it's linked to insurance) so alternative work has to be set – such as theory work, which can be seen as "boring".

Secondly, the regular teacher is off sick and has not sent in any work. So the work that you're delivering is not in line with what the pupils have been working on in their regular lesson.

In either situation the motivation of the pupils to do the work is going to be low. Sometimes you might be able to motivate the pupils by playing radio (through the internet) on the condition that they work, and work quietly. Younger pupils can be tempted to complete the work by the offer of a stamp or a sticker at the end of the lesson. Every class is different, the dynamics are not going to be the same – so to start with, its trial and error.

Be sympathetic to the pupils, remember how it felt to be given a piece of work, and it's clear to see it's a time waster

No!

This is a word that I try to avoid in lessons. It is negative, and not explanatory. As hard as it is, try to praise, this is called positive reinforcement. All pupils like attention, try to avoid paying attention to low level disruption (unless it's dangerous) but praise the pupils who are getting it right. Pupils will do anything to get attention.

Additionally, avoid over using the word NO! Eventually, pupils will just switch off. If you need to say no, then put it in the way of a sandwich. In this method, start with a positive, then the negative, and then, end the conversation on a lighter note. An example of this is, "haven't you done a lot of work? But I have noticed that..., but that can be changed if you..." This is the best way of saying no, because it's constructive.

When you're asking questions to the class, and some poor pupil is very enthusiastic but gets the question wrong. Once again, avoid saying no. In this situation, ask more questions to this pupil to encourage them to get to the right answer. For instance, "Why did you think that..., could there be another possibility? These open questions are to get pupils to think things through. Saying no to an enthusiastic pupil could harm their self-esteem and confidence.

> Remember you do not need to turn into a nagging wife like figure. Work hard to dodge the N word

Numeracy

Numeracy – like literacy is important. It is also something that you can embed in your cover lessons. For example if their drawing a table, or putting data into a graph.

As like literacy, numeracy can pop up in any subject. For example PE. If you've got 24 pupils how many teams of 4 will we have, or keeping score. A lot of pupils are using numeracy without even knowing it.

If I need a filler, I will play a game. I will choose a 4 digit number – I'll write it down to avoid allegations of cheating. Then I will draw 4 lines on the board, and ask a pupil to give me 4 numbers, and write these on the line (one number per line). I ignore any numbers that are not the ones I've personally picked. If the pupil's number is in the wrong place, I'll put a square around it, and a circle if it's the right number in the right place. The next pupil pick four numbers, using the information from the previous line. The aim is for the class to correctly guess my numbers, all in the right order. When they have it right, I show them what I have written down. The winner of the game can pick the next 4 digits. This is a great game to improve pupil's logical thinking.

Other games can be found on the internet, remember ideal games for a cover supervisor requires no time to set up or plan.

If your numeracy skills need brushing up, then do it. Otherwise you'll only get caught out, and that would only be embarrassing

Objectives

These are something the pupils expect to see at the start of each and every lesson. The objectives tell the pupils what they expect to get out of that lesson. These should be on the board at all times during the lesson.

In an ideal world, all this sounds great. Although as a cover supervisor within that one single sentence, that explains what the class is going to do for the entire lesson, the objective just magically disappears. With this in mind, it's up to you to think of one, below is a list of objectives that you can use.

Start with...

- At the end of the lesson, you will be able to...
- We are going to cover...
- Today, you will ...

And then...

- Understand how .... (plants need the sun to grow)
- Revise for the end of unit test
- Develop independent learning skills

You can mix and match these. Of course it depends on the actual subject and topic.

You don't have to use an objective, but it will help the pupils to focus. Additionally it will make you appear more professional in the classroom

Observations

Another reason why we might have to cover lessons is when heads of departments need to observe lessons taught by their teachers in their department. Teachers have a number of terms and conditions, one of which is being able to choose which lessons they are observed in (this excludes Ofsted observations). So heads of departments will need covering regularly.

As these are *planned* absences, cover work should be there. The other problem that you'll have, is that the pupils will be confused. They will have seen Ms Collins today, and will be expecting her to teach their lesson. Instead of repeating myself, I'll wait until all the pupils are present and then explain that their regular teacher is observing another teacher, and there may be every chance that they will be back towards the end of the lesson (so I suggest that you sit in your normal seating plan – is how I would finish that sentence).

Occasionally you will be observed. In this situation, show the observer the lesson plan. They will appreciate how hard you have to work to conduct the lesson, quickly think of ways to stretch the task, while managing the behaviour of the class. Chances are it will either be a teacher who doesn't fully understand the cover supervisor's role, or the cover manager who works in an office.

> If you get a chance, observe other staff, including both cover supervisors and teachers. You may learn a number of skills, and new tasks that you could use in your own cover lessons

Ofsted

Ofsted is the Office for Standards in Education, Children's Services and Skills. They inspect all educational providers, including nurseries, primary and secondary schools and colleges. After their inspection, the group of inspectors write a report and submit it to parliament. The school (in our case) is given the report with an overall grade. Below is a list of grades, and their meanings:

- Grade 1 The school is outstanding
- Grade 2 The school is good
- Grade 3 The school requires improvement
- Grade 4 The school is inadequate

Most schools are aiming to get at least a "good" if not better. When you get to grade 3, the school will be inspected more regularly. As for grade 4, Ofsted have a greater input, for instance teachers will have to submit their lesson plans.

When the school is hosting an Ofsted visit, it can be described as entering a different school. Everything is how it should be. As for cover, it will be light. Your cover manager may suggest to support in lessons, but teachers will not appreciate this, because they will not have taken additional support into account on their lesson plans. If they are being observed, they could be degraded by the Ofsted inspector.

In the unlikely event of being observed by Ofsted, show the inspector the lesson plan and ensure that you stick to the plan and keep the pupils safe

Parents, Carers & Guardians

Ok, in school we deal with pupils, however these pupils go by another name. It'll come as no surprise but at the end of the day we work with children. These children have parents, carers or guardians.

You need to be careful and remember this. Even when that pupil is trying to push your buttons to see if you flip. If you take the matter further, it can feel like hitting your head against a brick wall. Pupils can be very manipulative, their parents will of course believe their little dumpling, as he can't do anything wrong. With this in mind, you have to be whiter than white. If you're going to lose your temper, do it privately.

On the other hand, try to make positive contact with parents, carers and guardians. If you can, send a post card home or make a phone call to let the parents know how good their child has been. This is actually good PR for you, when you see that pupil again they will remember this, and will want to work harder for you. This is in line with positive reinforcement. There is more about this in the carrot versus stick section of this book.

You may be asked to attend a parents evening. Don't be nervous when meeting parents, they are just normal people. The chances are, parents will be just as nervous, as they're coming into school, the last time that they were in school could have been when they were a kid.

> The golden rule, don't talk to pupils in a way that you wouldn't talk to your own children

Personal security

This is rather important. We are in a society now, where pupils are quite smart and savvy. Based on what pupils say, it could cost you your job or even career. You have to be extremely careful, don't touch children in any way, this could be taken in the wrong way, do not allow yourself to be in a room alone with a pupil. If you have to talk to a pupil always have the classroom door open. This avoids any allegation that could be made. With this in mind, it is important to be in a union, they will protect you if this happens to you.

The other side of this is your personal belongings. If you can, leave your wallet, house and car keys and mobile phone in a safe place. I don't take these into class. When the class are working on their main task and I am circulating, my attention is on the class, not on my bag. Unfortunately some pupils will take advantage of your back being turned.

I work on a two bag system. I have my normal hand bag that contains house and car keys, make up and my phone. My second bag is the one I use for covering. In this bag I have everything I need for classes, and most importantly anything that goes missing or is damaged - it doesn't matter.

A classroom full of pupils can be a dangerous place. Be extremely careful, and look after yourself. Do not be placed in a situation that could be unsafe

Physical Disabilities

Yes, you will come across pupils with some sort of physical disabilities. I hope it goes without saying, that their disabilities do not affect their intelligence or ability to learn.

If a pupil arrives in a wheel chair, don't worry. If this is a classroom that they use weekly, the classroom will be organised to cater for their needs, with wide gangways.

If a pupil is deaf they may have hearing aids, and will not need additional assistance. Some pupils will need you to wear a device around your neck. This picks up on what you say, and reduces the other distracting noises. This goes straight to their personal hearing device. With this in mind, if you have a private conversation don't forget to turn it off! If not, the pupil could hear a confidential conversation.

With visual disabilities, there should be equipment in the room that the pupil can use. In all cases of pupils with physical disabilities, take the lead from the pupil. They will know what strategies are there for them.

Don't see the disabilities over the pupil. Do not be naïve, some of these pupils will use their disability to avoid doing work, or even misbehave. Treat these pupils exactly the same as other pupils, follow the behaviour policy. Some of these pupils may have a teaching assistant, they will know how to deal with these pupils.

> Consider the evacuation procedure, ensure that they are safely out if there is a drill

Policies

In every school that you work in, there will be policies for almost everything. Policies include data protection, safeguarding, admissions, homework, uniform, behaviour, staff dress code, SEN, staff appraisals, health and safety, Gifted and talented, child protection, and many more.

Policies are generated when the government produces guidelines that effect schools, or children. Each school will have to produce a policy in line with the government's whitepaper for that particular issue. With this in mind, every school will have a safeguarding policy (for example), but it will be different from their neighbouring schools. The policy will have to be personalized to fit the schools staffing structure, and their school building. Within the policy, it'll explain the procedures, for example who needs to do what, and when. But we must remember that policies are there to keep us all safe.

If you're working for an agency, it is unreasonable to read every policy ever written for that school (and find your room and locate the cover work) before the start of class. The cover manager will issue you with the most important policies such as the behaviour, and evacuation policy. If you regularly work in that school, you'll learn them after a little time. If you need assistance from other staff, the first thing that they'll ask is have you followed the policy?

> Love them or hate them, policies are here to stay. Read them, get to know them, and use them

Practical Lessons

Practical lessons include PE, wood work, food technology, textiles, and science. You will not be allowed to conduct a practical in these subjects. The school insurance will state for a practical lesson to be conducted, a specialist teacher has to be teaching. Some cover supervisors, may have a degree but will not be classed as a specialist in teaching that subject. Teachers of these subjects will have additional training in health and safety. This will help to prevent any accidents from happening.

When you cover a practical lesson, it will be theory based. Pupils do not like the idea of "writing" in a doing lesson. Expect some resistance when telling the pupils of the tasks.

Additionally, their regular teacher may have promised to do something special for this particular lesson, it could be an experiment, or getting the trampoline out. In both cases you can't do it, no matter how much the pupil's complain.

When introducing your lesson, it may help to explain that knowing *why* something happens, will help them when they actually do it. Using an example such as learning to drive, you need to know the high way code before you actually drive.

Brace yourself, for resistance. Resistance is better than having an accident in your lesson

Praise

It's a fact, pupils like praise, even the naughty ones! This works on the same principle as not saying no. If you can try to find ways of praising pupils (as difficult as it is), then do it.

Some behaviour policies work on this idea. One of the reasons why pupils behave badly because they want attention from the teacher. These pupils see any attention as good. If you can try to avoid low level behaviour, and praise only the well behaved pupils. These "good" pupils are often overlooked, and no attention is paid to these, because it gets taken by the naughty ones. These naughty pupils are clever, they will realise what you're doing, they will either step up their poor behaviour, then in which case they can be removed, or alternatively start to behave because they want the attention.

Unfortunately pupils do not receive enough praise, inside or outside of school. This could explain why so many children have low self-esteem and confidence issues. With this in mind, some pupils just don't know how to accept any form of praise. So if you want to give praise, it may be worth giving praise privately, just going up to the pupil (while others are working) and just saying it loud enough for them to hear. This will prevent the pupil the embarrassment, being seen as a teacher's pet. Giving the group praise (for instance at the end of the lesson) it is ok to publicly say it.

Praise should be given for academic reasons. Reasons include, neat hand writing, completing work and working well in a group

Pupil names

When I started as a cover supervisor, I could have needed this section. I am rubbish with names.

If there are on average 25 pupils in a class, and you have five lessons, you will see 125 pupils a day, over a period of 5 days, potentially that is 625 pupils a week. Even if you are based in just one school, it is impossible to learn all their names. You might know a few, that's because they have given you hassle every time you've see them. But on the whole, it's a difficult one. Pupils only have one name to remember, and that's mine.

When doing the register, some names may be unfamiliar and be difficult to pronounce. Pupils will know where they are on the register, in these cases they will be ready to correct you. Ask them to repeat it, thank them and continue the register. Sometimes, they may have a preferred name, normally it's at this time that they'll tell you. You may remember for next time, or not. If not, you'll just have the same conversation.

It's also advisable to get the pupil to raise their hand as you say their name. You'll learn some of their names this way. It also adds some weight, if you know some of their names – especially the naughty ones - at least you can report them. Without this they can do what they like, as their unaccountable. What's more if this fails, don't rely on other pupils to tell you their names because they may get bullied if they do.

Remember, tell them your name - It's only polite

Pupil Perspective

Yes, once upon a time, we were all school kids. I can remember what it meant by having a "supply". It was an excuse not to work, and to watch the "it" kids swap names and annoy the sub teacher. To be honest, I rather enjoyed it.

Another side of this, is when the pupils are expecting their regular teacher to be there and they're not. The absent teacher has their course work that should have been handed back this lesson. And as a result the pupils can't "continue with the work". This is one reason why pupils can become frustrated.

Another reason for pupils to become frustrated is when their regular teacher is absent from their lesson a lot. This happens with the higher ability pupils, they worry that their not going to cover the topics required so that they can get a good mark in their exams.

"Continue with work" this might annoy us the cover supervisor, but it can irritate the pupils as well. As we know pupils work at different speeds, the frustration comes from those pupils who have completed the work, and there is nothing more to do. Some of these may be gifted and talented and have the need to work and dislike doing nothing in a lesson.

> Accept that pupils will display their frustration at you, but it isn't personal. It's just that you are the only person that is available to talk to

Qualifications

Yes, you do need some qualifications to become a cover supervisor. However depending on who you ask, you'll get a different answer. The reason for this, is that it is a relatively new role, with no one route into it.

If you become a cover supervisor through promotion from being a teaching assistant then, QCF (NVQ) Supporting Teaching and learning at level 3 is adequate as you'll have valuable classroom experience.

If you enter the job through an agency, a degree is needed with an interest of progressing further in education. This makes sense, as you will display a certain level of intelligence.

There is a qualification that is specifically aimed at cover supervisors. It's a QCF (NVQ) course, titled Cover Supervision of Pupils in Schools, Level 3. It's a fairly new course, and not many employers are even aware it exists. I have completed it, and highly recommend it.

Other qualifications that are needed, are English and Maths at a good level. If not, you'll have pupils who are more advanced then you! Additionally, attending courses such as first aid, managing behaviour and even completing the HLTA course would be useful.

Once you've qualified, don't quit. The more qualified you are, the more opportunities you have. After doing cover, you may want to progress on to a teaching degree

Questioning

This is a good skill to have. If you ask pupils good open questions, it can add value to your lessons. In addition to this, it's good to use when you have no idea about the subject. If you can ask a question to a fairly smart pupil, they will tell you, and by "acting stupid", and continuing by asking follow up questions. The pupil will explain further. Below is an example of this.

"Who can tell me about how the Romans lived?" – because I have no idea

> "Well, sir they made concrete, and other stuff."

"How did they use the concrete? – Roads, maybe? I've no idea

> "Me, Sir!! They built the Pantheon! It even had a dome, I think?"

Furthermore, this is a useful strategy to use if you need to fill time. If a pupil isn't listening, you can ask them a question, and put them on the spot. The pressure from their peers should be enough to make them stop and listen to you.

At the start of the lesson, you will be bombarded with questions, such as are you taking us for this lesson? Where is our normal teacher? What are we doing today, Sir? Are we watching a DVD? I wait, and tell them all at once, it saves time saying it 25 times.

Questions are good! Try asking open rather then closed questions, the pupils will have to work harder

Reflective Journals

Reflective journals (or personal logs) are a useful tool. If you choose to do them, they allow you to analyse a lesson or task and let you evaluate how it went, what went well and how it could have been altered to make it better. It's a lot to ask to complete one for every lesson, but just keep a note on certain things, both good and bad.

They are designed to allow you to look back at your practice and think about how it went, so that you can build on it and improve. If you have done an NVQ you should be familiar on reflective journals and hopefully appreciate the benefits. Below is an example of a Reflective Journal.

"I've just had a year 9 class, low ability. I've come across this class before, but in another lesson. They were horrible then. Based on the last lesson, I decided to be positive as I figured they are always being shouted at all the time. I smiled as they entered the class, and praised the girls for sitting down quickly. Ryan (who I had to send out last time) was wanting my attention, I ignored his tapping, but when he raised his hand I spoke to him. I thanked him for his contribution. Wow! It worked. I didn't think it would. Next time, I'll try to encourage Ryan to hand out the books, he likes the praise."

It might be time consuming, but if you decide to go on to teaching, you'll have to do them then. Get in the practice now

Resources

Resources are anything that you may use in the classroom. This includes books, paper, pens, pencils and even the teaching assistant!

As a cover supervisor you cannot expect that everything you need will be available. I've known instances where the absent teacher has planned for the group to watch a DVD, while another teacher had taken the DVD because that teacher was absent! So teachers, who are not good at planning, will see an opportunity and take it! This is regardless of what is planned for the cover lesson. This is why I recommend having some basic resources, such as plain and lined paper, and coloured pens.

Other resources include the use of ICT. When pupils work on computers, the temptation is there to play games. With this you have to be extra vigilant, and ensure that they are working rather than playing. Additionally, be aware of the quick motion of their fingers when they "flick" between one screen and the other when you approach.

With the lesson plan, they should be a seating plan and a pile of resources that you should need for that lesson. However, back in the real world - if you require anything, the teacher next door should be able to offer assistance, either explaining where they are in the class room, or supplying them from their own room.

> If you need the resources for the lesson, do not be scared of asking for them, they should be their already

Rewards

Most schools have a behaviour system that focuses on rewards. So for example, some schools have a stamp system where if the pupils behave in your lesson, they will receive a stamp in their planner, and these are counted up and the pupil with the highest will win a prize at the end of the term.

Although, if you're an external cover supervisor, you may not have a stamp, or know what the exact criteria is for issuing the reward. With this in mind, there are other rewards that you can use. I purposely avoid issuing sweeties, as this can lead to problems – such as going against healthy schools protocol, and pupils having an allergic reactions.

Simple rewards can be having the radio on (some interactive white boards have speakers), as long as the pupils are working quietly. If their overall volume gets too loud, or a pupil misbehaves – the music goes off. As the majority of the class wants the music on, they will ensure that the naughty ones behave, a good use of peer pressure, wouldn't you say?

Another reward could be to play a game at the end of the lesson. The game can be something like hangman on the board, this strengthens their literacy skills.

Whatever reward is at hand, never reward for poor behaviour – this just sends out the wrong message "its ok to misbehave"

Role Model

Like it or not, you are a role model to pupils, although are you a good or bad role model? You may be an external cover supervisor, and have the attitude "these pupils are only going to see me once". The point is, for that one hour, pupils may just be revising, or continuing from the last lesson, but if you have the attitude of not bothering, they will adopt the same and not bother to do the work. Pupils can see a great deal, sometimes a lot more, then what we give them praise for. They can tell if you're there for the pupils, or just the money.

Within the pecking order of staff, cover supervisors are close to the bottom. We are seen as unqualified, and not very skilled, and for some teachers that is enough to treat cover supervisors not very professionally. We may get the worst classes, not very good work set but with that in mind, whatever problems we have with our colleagues, we must remain a positive role model.

Pupils are watching us all the time, to how we react to say a pupil swearing. If you over react and start swearing back (extreme – but I have seen it happen) this shows the other pupils how to deal with that as an adult. Alternatively, if you do nothing then that shows it's perfectly ok to swear. Getting the balance with this situation (and everything else) is vital.

> The minute you put a step wrong, you'll always be known as that "sub" who...

Routines

Children like routine. The very minute that they see a cover supervisor then the routine goes out of the window. This is the same, regardless if you work for the same school, or work for an agency.

It's to do with the really basic things, such as how the books are distributed, does one of the pupils hand them out, or do all pupils collect their own, or does the teacher place them in the pupils seating plan? In each classroom that the pupils enter, they will fall into the teachers little ways. So they may collect their own in maths, but have a book monitor in English.

As a cover supervisor you are never going to see the particular routine of their regular teacher, so it is important to adopt your own. There are two reasons for this, once the pupils see you (regardless of the lesson) they know *your* routine. And secondly, it'll make you feel more comfortable if you follow your own little ways. For example, I place the books out on a table near the door, and ask the pupils to pick up their own as they pass. This avoids all the hassle of who, what, where…, and it also gets the lesson off to a good start. Your routine, goes hand in hand with how you expect the class to behave. If you operate in a business-like manner, this will rub off on the pupils.

> How do you feel, when your routine is broken? Pupils see life in a microscopic way. Replacing their teacher is massive

Safeguarding

Knowing about safeguarding and our role within it is vital. Any person who works with children (and vulnerable adults) has to comply with the guidelines. This includes, all school staff, medical professionals and social workers. Each school will have their own policy based on the information from the government.

The policy will typically include information on what is the procedure for notifying the correct person who can deal with a concern about a child. Additionally, explaining the responsibilities of each member of staff and how they should operate in line with safeguarding.

Safeguarding ensures that children (and vulnerable adults) are safe while in your care. For cover supervisors, this means that wires are tucked away, and bags are completely under their tables in classrooms. However given the role of the cover supervisor, this can be difficult to maintain, when you're unfamiliar to the classroom. Identifying pupils can be an issue. An idea could be, to ask the cover manager to print off the photos of the pupils in the class, and then you can match up the pupils to their names. With this, I must point out that this document must be destroyed once you've finished with it. Shredding is advisable. This document could be dangerous in the wrong hands, as it identifies children. This is a safeguarding issue in itself.

> If you are an external cover supervisor, do not forget to sign in, and where the badge that the school office issue to you

Sanctions

During this book I have encouraged you to be positive and reward rather than sanction. However, sometimes the behaviour of a pupil is so bad or is dangerous that you have no other option but to issue a sanction. For example, if a pupil has physically assaulted another pupil, than a sanction has to follow, and has to equal the behaviour. In any case, always follow the procedure. This helps with consistency. Ideally pupils should know that if they do…, they expect …. To happen, this is regardless of the subject or staff.

If you are going to sanction the pupils, ensure that you are allowed to perform that particular task and that you are prepared to do it yourself. Even if that means losing your break to do the detention. If you don't follow through with the sanction that you set, pupils will discover this and will learn that you don't mean it, and continue to behave in the same way that you don't want them to.

Find out exactly what the procedure is for cover supervisors, as they are often over looked when sanctions are introduced. Are you expected to do detentions? If so, do you get paid for them? If not, who do you notify? Are you allowed to make phone calls home? Is there a script that you are meant to follow? Do you have time during the day to make these calls?

Match the sanction to the behaviour. Even removing the pupil into another room, maybe enough to calm them down

Sanity

Try to keep hold of it, if you can. This is linked with keeping calm, and not getting stressed. However, I am convinced that cover supervisors do have one of the most stressful roles within school. It's a possibility that every lesson that you cover will be a challenge.

If you've had a bad lesson, and you're straight into another lesson, do not let it show to the new class. If you do, the new class will only "feed" off your stress and in turn kick up a fuss. If you're short tempered and flustered, they will see it and retaliate, and this will make you feel even more stressed. If you can draw a line under the previous lesson, and start a fresh in the second lesson. If you need to follow up something, then do it when you have calmed down. If you can talk to another cover supervisor, ask for their perspective. Doing this will allow you to reflect and think more clearly.

If you do get stressed (and it's perfectly normal to), accept that you work as a cover supervisor, and it can be difficult at times, but nip it in the bud and talk to somebody. Maybe the cover manager (but remember, they are only office based) is unware a particular problem. It could be as easy as keeping you based in one side of the school, rather than having you run from one side of the school to another for every lesson. Or keeping you out of English - because you hate the subject.

If you can put your hand on your heart and say that you have done you're best, even in the worst of your lessons, then you can keep your head held high. You've done your best

Seating Plans

In this idealistic world that we talk of, where lesson plans are left neatly on the desk with all the resources required, you'll also find a seating plan. This mythical document tells you where each pupil sits within the classroom.

Right, back to the real world. In my time as a cover supervisor, I would say that only 1% of lesson plans, are accompanied with a seating plan. These are just as important as the lesson plan. All teachers will have a seating plan for each of their lessons, it's a requirement of Ofsted. The reason behind these plans is to either group the same type of pupils together (such as EAL and G&T pupils) or to have a mixture of pupils on each table. Equally, certain pupils will have been separated from each other, because they struggle to work when their together, or they cause trouble.

The only way you can ensure that all the pupils are sat where they are supposed to, is by asking the teaching assistant, but not every class comes with a teaching assistant. The other way is to listen out for "that" pupil to say extra loudly, "you're sat in my seat". Upon hearing that, you can ask them all to go to where they are meant to be sat. You will never get the seating plan 100% right. If youre based in the same school, you'll know the characters that will course you trouble, and split them up.

Even if you have a seating plan, it may not be correct. The plan may have been drawn up at the start of term, and it was only last lesson when Louise now sits with Brenda - because they work well together

Sense of Humour

To work in any school, having a sense of humour is essential. In any high pressure job such as working in a school or a hospital "having a laugh" helps to let off steam.

Within the classroom, use your sense of humour very sparingly. You have to remember that not everybody has the same funny bone as you. What you find funny, will not make everybody else smile. If you make a joke with pupils, you have to be careful that the joke could not be seen as insulting by anybody in the class (for example the Irish, an Irish man enters a bar...) and that some pupils don't get carried away and start enjoying themselves too much. If a pupil wants to tell you a joke, then let them but ask, is it appropriate to tell that joke to an adult? Most of the time their innocent and sometimes can even make you smile.

The staffroom is where you can let off some steam. However with this in mind, taking the micky about certain pupils (or staff) is not advisable or professional. However, smiling at a piece of work that a year 6 has done is ok.

Of course there are times that your sense of humour is out of the question. For example, telling a pupil off when they have done something wrong (but you can see the funny side), but for professional reasons you can't smile, and when they tell an inappropriate joke that you found funny.

> Yes, enjoy yourself, but remember that not everybody sees the world in the same light as you

Silence!

The only time that I ask for silence is when I am doing the register. With the excitement of having somebody different to their regular teacher, silence can be hard to get. One way of getting silence is to stand at the front of the class, cross armed while looking at your watch. Within a short time the class will be a wash of "shhh!", then if the lesson backs on to a break tell the class that the class will be making back the time in their own time. Another method that I use is to use a whistle (that I use for PE as well). This usually does the trick quite well.

Shouting that you need silence will only make the pupils talk louder, as mentioned before, just look at your watch or (if you can), put a timer on the interactive white board and let it tick. Most pupils will be familiar with this and will soon fall silent. If the pupils talk while you are, start up the timer and let it run until their quite again. This is part of my little routine, some older pupils have learnt just not to talk while I am.

As the national curriculum stands, it encourages pupils to talk and swap ideas. So asking the pupils to work in silence can be an unrealistic request, because firstly they may not be used to it and secondly the work may ask them to work in pairs or small groups.

Some teachers may set a test for the pupils to do in their absence, believing that it'll be easier for the cover supervisor. Getting the pupils to be quite for a whole lesson, can be draining, this can be just as hard work as a normal lesson

SIMS

Or to give it, its full name the **School Information Management System.** This is a computer system that has all the details of all the pupils, and all staff. It includes the timetable of all pupils and staff, and is the system that your cover manager will work on when organising cover. If you believe that your cover manager only gives you the "dodgy" classes, then think again. All that they see is a series of classes that require covering. In the past I have had more or less the same class for two consecutive lessons, once for English and another for Maths. This has been a fluke, not intentional from the cover manager.

If you have access to this system on the computer, there are a few rules that you have to follow. One of which is that you shouldn't leave the computer "open" when SIMS is loaded. If you have to walk away from the computer, it should be locked. This goes back to safeguarding, all it takes is a pupil to search for another pupil and they will have access to all their personal details including medical requirements, and contact details.

Another rule is that you should never put SIMS up on the interactive white board. Once again this infringes on safeguarding. It may show that one pupil is absent for a personal reason, or has a note beside their name.

Before you set foot in the class as a cover supervisor, you should receive some training on SIMS because if you enter the information incorrectly the implications could be massive.

SIMS – if in doubt, ask

Snow

Snow has magic tendencies within school. It can send the most normal child scatty.

If it snows overnight, expect to be busy during the day. You may struggle in, only to be told that school is closed, or that it opens later to allow staff to arrive in. Once school is operational, there is still a chance that school could be closed early due to further snow fall during the day.

It's a fact that snow will happen at some point, but the exact date and time is unknown. With this in mind it is important to have a plan for snow, before it happens. For example, if it is forecast for snow, plan to walk in if you can, and take your school clothes in a bag (including shoes). Or if you drive, have a blanket ready to place over the windscreen, or double check the bus times. It's a fact you may be late into school, but let school know of the approximate time you expect to be in.

Once in school, it will be all hands on deck, you may be asked to take a group of pupils and "just do something". This will allow the senior leadership team to assess the current situation and assess the forecast during the day. Things that influence a school closure, includes if the buses are going to finish early, and pupils may need them to get home, and the severity of the on-going snow.

> If you have to cover a mixed group of pupils - take a paper register, and send it down to the office. This is safeguarding (again) but once the school know how many pupils are in they can make an informed decision

Smart Board

The smart board is a piece of technology that is linked up to the computer which will allow PowerPoints to be shown, and to show clips of DVD's. In addition to this, it can be used in the same sense as a white board, where it can be written on (and saved).

Teachers use this a lot, they can plan their lessons at home, and present the lesson through a PowerPoint. Or use the functions that the smart board package comes with. It is very child friendly, but can take a little time to get confident with both the software and hardware – but it is worth it.

As for a cover supervisor, getting to grips with this is vital. You can set up pages where you can just input the date, title of the lesson and task on the smart board, this allows you to look more "professional" and the pupils will be more accepting. If you have time, look through the other functions. I like the timer, I use this to prove how long that I have been waiting for the pupil's attention. This is a method that teachers use, so the pupils are familiar to it, and fall silent rapidly. The pupils like the smart board because it is visual (learning styles) and in most cases has been used since they were in primary school.

If training is available, take it with both hands! The smart board, has many functions and features that can really make a massive difference to a cover supervisor.

If you have a free lesson, experiment with it. See what you can and can't do with it. It will improve your delivery of the lesson

Special Educational Needs

The definition of a pupil with Special Educational Needs (SEN), is a pupil who has a barrier to learning. A barrier could be what we traditionally consider as SEN such as Dyslexia or ADHD. However, other barriers include EAL pupils and even those pupils who are G&T. Each group of pupils have a barrier, but is very much different to other groups.

I talk from personal experience, and see each pupil as a pupil, and then the problem. A lot of these pupils, who have a particular need will also be intelligent, articulate and not stupid. In the majority of cover lessons that you cover, you may not even know who has a special need.

When it comes to covering a lesson with pupils who have SEN, the absent teacher may not have even considered the requirements of these pupils. The work that is set, may be difficult for these pupils to complete. So you may have to differentiate by outcome. So for example, the G&T may have to complete all the work plus the extension, and the SEN pupils may only have to complete task one and two, where the EAL pupils have to find the meanings of the key words in their first language. When differentiating, don't publicly announce it, float and quietly tell each pupil of your expectations of the amount of work you expect them to complete.

Be very wary of pupils who state that they have special needs, because they may be just getting out of doing the work!

Staffroom

This is the place where you can relax a little, before you battle onwards.

However, within this sanctuary if you're not careful, you can upset a lot of staff. Within this room, long standing staff will have their seat, where they have always sat since the school opened many years ago. The other thing you have to be careful of, is the cup you use for your brew. If you cross the wrong person, you could upset them for the rest of the week!! If you are an external cover supervisor, bring your own cup, it just saves the hassle.

Some staff rooms may be locked by either a normal lock, or a maglock. Generally speaking you'll be safe to keep your personal stuff here. Nevertheless, if it's not locked - anyone can go in it (including pupils). If this is the case, then do not leave anything here, it may just disappear.

Generally speaking, it's not a place I spend a lot of time in. I personally prefer to use the time to get my head around my next lesson, especially if it's at the other side of the school. I can log on to the computer, log in to SIMS and read through the lesson plan, or locate a teacher to ask for work. As I have previously said, I like to set the books out at a table nearest the door, it's part of my routine. Losing part of my break, or lunch is worth it as I don't need to panic and do everything all at once. I can relax knowing my lesson is organized.

If you need to let off steam, this is the place to do it

Start of the lesson

If you can get the start of the lesson off ok, then hopefully the rest of the lesson will be. This is the busiest part of the lesson, you have to get to the classroom, log on to the computer, read the cover lesson (if it's there), while it almost seems every pupil asks either – are you taking us for this lesson, or what are we doing?

This is a unique problem that supply teachers and cover supervisors have. When teachers plan for their lessons they do not take this into account as they know the pupils, the classroom and the subject. You'll find that teachers will either write next to nothing, or write an essay - which is full of waffle and is time consuming to read.

If you have been given a starter for the class to do, get them to do it as soon as they walk through the door. This will allow you to do what you need to do. As for the numerous questions, politely ask them to take a seat and you'll explain to all of the pupils when they are settled.

If you haven't been given a starter by the absent teacher, this is where it is useful to have a couple up your sleeve. As you cover other lessons, you may come across starters that you could use in other lessons.

> Once again, if you have a free lesson, it may be worth searching for some starter activities that you can use at a moment's notice

Stereotyping

Stereotyping is when you look at a person, and make a judgement about them based on how they look. This is something that you cannot do in school. For example a group of year 11 boys may look daunting, but they could be well mannered and open the door for you when your hands are full.

Additionally, the really scruffy kid who never gets picked for captain at sport could be on the G&T register for maths. You have to treat every child the same, regardless of how they look.

Preventing stereotyping in the classroom, is important. Such comments such as "people who have red hair, are hot tempered" should be dealt with immediately. Stereotyping can lead to discrimination and racial comments, both of which have no place in a classroom.

On the other side, pupils will be making a judgement about you. Have you got tattoos, piecing's or an unusual haircut? It's these things that make people unique and gives them a sense of identity. However when working in schools, we have the image of the school to bear in mind. So this may mean covering up the tattoos and removing the facial piecing's. If giving up who you are, is a problem - it may be worth considering if this is the job for you.

What would people think about how you dress at school, does it fit in the corporate image of the school?

Stick to your Guns

When you are stood at the front of the room trying to explain the task. And that solitary hand goes up, where the pupil asks if they can go to the toilet, Mr Palmer? At this point you should say No! This can either be a work avoidance method, where their need to "go", will disappear when you continue to refuse them permission. On the other hand, they may really want to "go". You should still encourage them to wait until break time. Only let them go, if they have a toilet pass on the account of having a medical problem.

If you cave in and let them go, what does this tell the pupils? It shows that you're a push over, and if they persevere you'll change your mind eventually. Pupils are very good at reading people and will know who is a push over. Other than excusing pupils to go to the loo, it has larger consequences. If you have to sanction a pupil it will not hold the same weight as it would with another cover supervisor who sticks to what they say.

Pupils may not like you when you deny them of going to the toilet, but they will respect you for it eventually, and know to not to ask in future lessons. As I have previously mentioned in the book, it is all about being consistent. Pupils like structure, they like to know where they stand with staff.

If you say one thing, and then back track – this can be confusing. Part of the cover supervisors role, is to communicate well, and this means sticking to your guns

Strike (Industrial Action)

This is an interesting one. If you belong to a union, you may be asked to go on industrial action. Of course you have a choice if you go out on strike, but you will not get paid for the time out protesting. You have to decide if the reason for striking is worth the sacrifice. If in doubt talk to either your union representative or your local union branch.

Teachers can also go on strike, and is normally to protest about their working terms and conditions. These strikes, have a set of rules that schools have to obey. For example, both supply teachers and cover supervisors, should not cover a striking teacher's lessons. The striking teacher should not set work for the lessons that they're going to miss. The reason for such rules, is to course as much disruption as possible. If there isn't enough teachers in the school, then the school will have to close, and this disruption will spread to parents. In turn parents may have to place their child(ren) in to child care or have to take time off work, often without pay.

With up and coming strikes, schools have started to think outside the box with this problem. For instance, the school may choose to close to the younger year groups, and only allow the higher years to have catch up days to concentrate on completing their course work. This is one for the schools, but it won't be long before the unions renews the terms and conditions and put a stop to "catch up days".

| Never cover for a striking colleague. You can refuse |

Supply Teachers

Supply teachers are not cover supervisors. Both roles are different. Supply teachers are qualified teachers, they will have a degree in teaching, such as a Cert Ed or PGCE. Because supply teachers are more qualified, they will get paid more than a cover supervisor. With this, they are expected to teach the pupils. And please note, they will encounter the exact same problems as cover supervisors, if no work has been set.

Supply teachers must be used on the fourth day of the teacher's absence. The idea behind this, is that cover supervisors are for short term cover only, where no formal teaching is conducted. After this the pupils must have a teacher to progress their learning.

However, supply teachers may be used for odd days, or even take cover supervisor's assignments, if no supply teacher work is available. Of course this agreement has to be agreed between the teacher and their agency.

Talk to supply teachers, they are the nearest people who know what you have to endure. It is advisable to swap ideas regarding covering lessons. They may offer you help and advice in what resources and techniques to use in the classroom.

Traditionally, supply teachers have been seen as strange people who do supply work. As like cover supervisors, being a supply teacher, offers flexibility – ideal for personal commitments

Taking Control

When you're stood at the front of the classroom, you are the one who should be in control. This can be a difficult concept to accept if you have been a teaching assistant.

As a teaching assistant, the teacher takes the lead and makes all the decisions for the lesson. The teaching assistant just does what there told. If you have been a teaching assistant that has been given a promotion to a cover supervisor, it can be quite mind boggling. Even though you know the pupils, the class room, it can be a little daunting when you realize that you have no one else in the classroom to call on. Over time this feeling will disappear, and will be replaced with confidence.

The other way of getting into the role, is by walking straight into a vacancy either at a school or with an agency. If you haven't had any classroom experience, it can seem a little intimidating. Normally your employer will offer you some training.

Whichever way you enter the role, you still have to adopt the same attitude. Ok you may not be a teacher, but you still have the same expectations. For instance when you ask for quiet, you get it, that when you give out any sanctions - they are taken seriously, and that when you tell the class to do something – they do it. No, if or buts, they just do it.

Practice makes perfect

Teaching Assistants

Teaching assistants can vary in skills and efficiency. The majority of teaching assistants (TA) have chosen the role to fit in with their family needs - the work pattern coincides with their children's school holidays, while others see the role as a start in their career.

A good TA can be a life saver. They will tell you which pupils you need to look out for, and can confirm if the pupils are sat in the correct seating plan. When working with a TA, the attitude that you should have is that you should work together- work as a team. The TA will know the class, they will be supporting in that class most of the time, use the TA to your advantage. The TA will also know how the class behave for their regular teacher, and will be happy to prompt the pupils into behaving better.

However, a bad TA can make your lesson hard work. In the past, I have had TA's talk over me, when I have asked for the class to be quiet, others have undermined me, and one even told some of the class the wrong instructions! So what do you do? In the first instance, bite your tongue. Secondly, be the professional one, do not make a big deal of it in front of the class. If you need to say something to the TA, be tactful and do it privately.

| Work as a team, it'll be a better lesson |

Teaching Styles

You may think that this is a little odd to include, however I think it is important to consider. As a cover supervisor, you should not be teaching as such, but you should adopt a teaching style. Your teaching style depends a lot on your personality, both have to be compatible

This is something you can experiment with, and see which style suit you. I try to be quite formal, I expect the same standards as their regular teacher, for instance not accepting any swearing. Once I have taken the same class a few times, and they know what I expect of them, I can become a little more informal. Although the formal me, is never far away.

Another style, is to be quite friendly. Some cover supervisors use this, for some it works and others it doesn't. For this to work the pupils have to respect you and like you as a cover supervisor. If the cover supervisor is not well liked amongst the pupils, and the cover supervisor knows this, be friendly can come over as being fake and may do more harm than good. If this is the case, it doesn't take long for a reputation to develop.

Whichever style you choose, you have to be fair and professional. At the end of the day, your aim is to ensure that the set work gets done, and your life is made as easy as possible, this can be achieved by getting the pupils on your side and cooperating.

Research teaching styles, find one that fits you and your personality

Team Player?

For your day to run smoothly, you need to rely on a lot of staff to play their part. For example the cover manager to let you know if there are any changes to your day, the TA to help and support you as much as possible, the teacher who is absent (or another teacher) to set appropriate work for the lessons that your covering, and the behaviour staff to take care of the badly behaved pupils. Of course, cover managers, TA's, and behaviour staff may be absent from their role (it isn't only teachers who get sick), this puts stress on the rest of the school. Most of these roles do not get cover, but the rest of their team have to work harder to make up the short fall. This is where some things get over looked.

The majority of problems that cover supervisors encounter, can be traced back to another staff not playing their part. For example the cover manager not passing on a message, or the teacher doesn't provide cover work. In an ideal world, the role would be easier if everyone did their job. Cover supervisors are often seen as invisible, when they are doing their job well. When the absent teacher returns, their biggest issue is not to thank the cover supervisor(s) who covered them but to try and get up to speed with school life.

Of course cover supervisors have to play their part in being a team player, by ensuring that they perform their role and that they follow the schools policies and procedures.

Don't lose your temper if staff are not playing their part, you don't know what pressures they are up against

Technology

This section may produce goose bumps on your skin as you consider this section to be terrifying! But something you must understand, schools have to be at the forefront of technology. As they are producing adults of the future, and they need to be able to use both software and hardware that their chosen career requires. For some of these pupils, what they eventually choose may not even exist yet. For instance, the role of the cover supervisor did not exist when I left school. The world is advancing at a remarkable rate, and as cover supervisors we have to accept that.

In some schools, they have just as many computers as they have pupils. A useful device that is being used, is that of the humble tablet, EAL pupils use these to translate words. SEN pupils use apps that are more interactive and are more visual.

Technology even effects traditional subjects, such as Wood work, where pupils can design their ideas on a programme call Computer Aided Design (CAD). This programme is widely used in the engineering industry.

There is one piece of technology that you have to be careful of, and it's the humble mobile phone. Most phones have camera and video functions. These can be dangerous in the wrong hands. To avoid being caught out, insist that pupils put these away.

If you're not confident on computers, just have a tinker. The more time you're on them the better you'll feel

Timing

You have probably herd comedians go on about how important timing is. The same can be said in lessons. For example the register has to be done in the first 10 minutes of the lesson, and that you have to allow enough time for the class to tidy up the classroom before the bell goes.

From the minute you step in the building, the most useful piece of Equipment that you'll need is a watch. You'll also need to know how long each lesson is, how much time you have for lunch and of course what time is home time.

In regards of covering lessons, you will have to work out how long to spend on each task, and at what time to pack up. This is important because you will have to ensure that all the work that has been set is completed. For example I would allow maybe 10 to 15 minutes on the starter and then 30 minutes on the main activity, followed by 10 minutes for the plenary which will allow 5 minutes to tidy up. Each lesson is going to be different, and some lessons require a longer time to tidy up, such as art. Other exceptions include PE, in this case allow 10 minutes at the start and at the end of the lesson so that the pupils can change their clothing.

Your timing may need to change depending on how quick the pupils do the work, and if you have a fire drill. Your timings will never be set in stone.

Remember, time flies when you're having fun. This is equally true for you and the pupils

Trips, Visits & Residentials

The chances are, you will be left to cover the classes that have been left by the teacher, who are out on a field trip. Typically this happens by such departments such as geography. With this in mind, this department is going to be good at setting work. In some of these lessons, they may only be a few pupils in the class, because the rest of the pupils are out on the trip. If this is the case, you have an easy lesson, so enjoy it.

If you are lucky enough to go out on a trip, remember that you are still working. In my experience, trips tend to be harder than staying in school. If the trip is for educational purposes, the day should be structured, and you (along with other staff) will be their just as crowd control, for example making sure that the pupils behave correctly.

If the trip is a rewards trip, this is going to be less structured and the pupils are going to want to "do their own thing" at the theme park. You may be asked to do a duty at the meeting point, and tick off pupils as they "check in". At this meeting point, there will be a first aider – just in case.

In both cases you may get back to school later. Do not expect to get paid over time for this, as it is classed as a perk of the job.

On either type of trip, you and the pupils are still representing the school. So, do not do anything that will embarrass yourself or cause you to get into trouble. You're still working, and need to remain professional

Unions

I suggest very strongly that you join a union. They give you protection. For example many schools are changing into academies. The implication is that these academies are seen as a business, and operate differently. For instance some academies will outsource support staff. Unions do not like this, and will fight for your rights for your terms and conditions not to change, as in most cases they will not change to benefit you. This is exactly the same as teachers unions, they fight to protect their members to retain their pay and pensions. To join a union it will cost a few pounds every month, but it is worth it.

The other use that unions have, is that if a pupil has an allegation about you, your union will represent you. They will ensure that you are advised on what to do, and one of their representatives will attend meetings with you. Schools may be a big organization, but do not always get things right. As a single voice you may not be heard, but with a union behind you, you can ensure that you will be treated fairly.

In addition to this, when you join a union, they will offer you benefits for joining. These benefits include cheaper car and home insurance for members, free training and in some cases financial assistance, and health care costs, such as dentistry and eye care.

If you are not a member of a union, then I suggest you do it. You never know what may happen, pupils can be very manipulative and some know the damage that they can course for a person's career

Uniforms

Most schools will have a uniform, and will insist on that all pupils were it. It is part of your responsibility to check that the uniform is being worn by all pupils correctly. Secondly school aged pupils are constantly trying to push the boundaries and possibly ware trainers instead of shoes, or loosen the ties when it should be snug around the neck. This is normal for teenagers to boycott the school rules.

When pupils see a cover supervisor, they will believe that the lack of their uniform will be ignored. If you want to be taken seriously, and remember you have the same expectations as the regular teacher, you must tackle the uniform issue.

In an ideal world, you can check the uniform as you stand at the door, greeting the pupils into your lesson. However, this doesn't always happen.

If you notice that a pupil isn't wearing the right uniform, do not make a big fuss about it, but approach them when the class is on task and ask them to change. You may have to give them a note to leave the classroom. Once again, it's all about balance, not stopping the class from working but still getting that one pupil to conform to the school rules.

> If you are stuck for a lesson activity, turn this into a task. Either have a debate or get the pupils to write reasons for and against pupils to ware uniform. Most pupils feel passionately about this, and normally generates good work

Useful Skills

As a cover supervisor, you may not teach pupils academically, however as a cover supervisor there are many things we can pass on to these pupils.

The art of negotiation is a useful skill, when covering. They will try to get out of doing any work. If you can convince them to do some work then you've won.

Listening is vital. As cover supervisors, we can learn a lot from the pupils, they may be only children but they have interests and information that we don't know. If we can listen to them, it helps to build a good relationship.

Another skill that is useful, is to be open minded. Listening to the pupils may cause you to consider doing things differently. Just because their young doesn't mean that their ideas are any less valued. Children see things in a different light to adults.

Keeping calm, and not getting flustered. Some pupils take great delight in trying to get both supply teachers and cover supervisors alike in losing it. Either ignore it, or remove the pupil from the room.

With all this in mind, the biggest thing that pupils pick up is the social skills, how to communicate to different types of people, and how to deal with unexpected changes such as a change of staff for their lessons.

| All these are life skills that can benefit us all in our day to day life |

Voice

Your voice is one of the most important tools that you have. Using your voice efficiently does take time, which is the same as teachers. Newly qualified teachers struggle with this too.

When talking about the voice, there are two things that we have to consider. The first is the volume, and the second is the tone. When both of these factors work well, this tool that you have has an amazing effect on the pupils.

The volume, is important. It is all too easy to shout, I've done it myself. In some cases it doesn't work, the pupils just talk louder. If you're shouting to get their attention, put the timer on the interactive white board, and quietly wait. The longer you wait, the longer they have to wait at break time. This is a visual way, and also protects your voice. If you don't believe me, try it.

The tone that you use is just as important as the volume that you use. The tone is **how** you say what you need to. This requires some practice, learning how to be serious, tell a pupil off, and even show your disgust at how the class have behaved. It is worth observing other staff (both cover supervisors and teachers) and watching how they use theor voice.

As silly as it is, practice in front of the mirror, or even with your own children. Experiment with both volume and tone. And remember a little can go a long way

Weather

This may seem a strange one to include, as the weather is outside and most lessons are held inside, but read on.

- In cold weather, pupils will be resistant to take their coats off when in lesson, even though the heating is on.
- In hot weather, it will be hard to motivate pupils to work because it's "too warm". Pupils asking to be excused can be a problem (and also going to the toilet)
- Snow. Sends even the most level headed pupil into a frenzy of excitement. It's difficult to get them to concentrate.
- When it is raining, pupils will play up if they cannot go outside, and let some steam off. If they do escape, their will end up sitting in cold wet clothes – and will not work.
- The sun may also course problems too. If the classroom you're in hasn't any blinds, then either the pupils or you may struggle if the sun dazzles you.
- The wind, it makes pupils silly and behave in a hectic fashion. This has actually been given its own name, which is Nature Deficit Disorder.

Some pupils will use the weather as an excuse to not work. In the real working world, regardless of the weather, we all have to work, and this is the same message that we have to pass on to our pupils

Websites

These can be your biggest aid. However you will have to search on sites aimed at teachers. If there is anything in this book that you are unsure of, then goggle it. I have only touched some topics very lightly. One thing that I must point out, is to always question the information you read, how reliable is the information, has the site referenced their sources?

The internet can provide you with a lot of ideas on lesson activities, ideas and resources. If you can try and get organized. To save time, if you have found a good website, save the address on to Microsoft word with a brief description. Do this will save you time when you want to find it again or want to print off more work sheets.

Whatever you find, share it with the rest of the cover supervisors. They might use it, or not – it's up to them. The internet is so big that it may be difficult to find the same website without some assistance.

If you are showing the class something on the internet through the interactive white board, freeze the board until you have found what you are looking for. This prevents pupils seeing content that may not be suitable for children. Some subjects are pretty close to the bone. For example "taking drugs", and "sex education", in both cases you can only imagine what both phrases can bring up.

Use your free lessons to search on the internet, you never know what you might find

Worksheets (or paper aeroplanes)

Some lessons you will be bombarded with work sheets. You will have a worksheet for the starter, the main activities and then possibly another sheet for the plenary.

Teachers set worksheets, as they believe that it's going to be easier for the cover supervisor, and in some ways they are easy – just hand them out and away they go.

However with worksheets, they do have their down sides. You may be expected to do the photocopying. As a cover supervisor, it is not your role to prepare resources for the lessons that you are covering. But you are over a barrel, if you do it, you might be expected to do it all the time, but if you don't – you've no work for the lesson that you're covering. In this situation, do the copying because entertaining a group of pupils for an hour without any work can be exhausting and stressful.

The other problem that you may encounter is that the pupils will use the sheets of paper to make aeroplanes, or scrunch them up into balls and throw them at other pupils. These pupils may want to "play in the game", while other pupils may just want to get their heads down and do the work. The problem with this, that you can't remove the balls or aeroplanes because you'll be removing their work. See the problem? You just need to put up with it.

> When collecting in worksheets, ensure that pupils put their names on each sheet, this will ensure that the regular teacher will know who has done what work

ZZZZ

Falling asleep during your lessons should be impossible. Every day is different, and will certainly keep you on your toes. The advantage the cover supervisors have over their teaching colleagues is that cover supervisors can sleep easy. Whereas teachers will know what classes they have the following day, and may worry that it's "that awful" group again. With cover supervisors, yes you may have awful groups to cover, you never know. Its only when you see that class code on the cover list, then it's too late to worry about it. At this point it's a matter of just getting on with it. In my experience, with these awful lessons, the time goes quickly, so before you know it the lesson is over.

Although, with this in mind, it is vital that you have a good night sleep. If you're tired, and stressed and pupils are nagging at you it can leave you feeling irritated and bad tempered. You know the amount of sleep that is right for you, to operate properly at school.

In some instances, you will have pupils who will fall asleep in your lessons. This may reflect on you, but the chances are (especially with teenagers) their sleep patterns go a little crazy. I've known mostly boys stay up playing on the latest computer game on their console, and before they know it, its 4 in the morning. Girls don't escape sleepless nights either, with the invention of social networks they can be on their computers for hours.

Never underestimate a good night's sleep

Printed in Great Britain
by Amazon.co.uk, Ltd.,
Marston Gate.